THE GLORY OF GOD

Demetrius Battle

Copyright © 2024 Demetrius Battle

All rights reserved

The characters and events portrayed in this book are fictitious. Any similarity to real persons, living or dead, is coincidental and not intended by the author.

No part of this book may be reproduced, or stored in a retrieval system, or transmitted in any form or by any means, electronic, mechanical, photocopying, recording, or otherwise, without express written permission of the publisher.

ISBN-13: 9798323731206

Cover design by: Art Painter
Library of Congress Control Number: 2018675309
Printed in the United States of America

To my Lovely wife Amanda

CONTENTS

Title Page
Copyright
Dedication
Introduction
Chapter One   1
Chapter Two   14
Chapter Three   41
Chapter Four   76
Chapter Five   103
Bibliography   128
Acknowledgement   129
Books In This Series   131

INTRODUCTION

The assemblies (Congregations) in America have been passive for generations when it concerns God's kingdom agenda. This of course does not apply to all the assemblies, but a great percentage. We've allowed the affairs of the world to divide us and even conquer us. Politics, doctrinal beliefs, cultural differences, race and many more. But the bridegroom calls out to His bride. The Shepherd cries out to His sheep. The head of His own body calls out to the members thereof, to properly align itself. God is performing a clerical call to all His people in this hour. A Vocational call to the church that remains in the land in the last days. We are in the last days and the prophecy written in Joel has not changed.

The prophecy that concerns a generation walking in the power of Yahweh's spirit, and the signs being revealed in the heavens and earth. Signs that consist of blood, fire, and billows of smoke. Signs that consist of the moon turning to blood and the sun refusing to shine. The great day where the POWER of God will shake the very heavens and the earth. As a mighty wind from a storm shakes the leaves off a fig tree. Such prophecy is not yet fully fulfilled. It did not stop after the days the first century church departed the scene. It did not cease when the 12 Apostles, the mighty evangelists, disciples, and even the great apostle Paul left the scene. No. but the prophecy is still relevant to this day. It still belongs to you and your children. It still belongs to the people of God that make up his assemblies.

The LORD is calling us to sanctify ourselves. He's calling us to align ourselves. The Lord has a plan and a great purpose for His church in this hour. The world is getting darker, and sin is growing. Wickedness is abounding more, and the love of man has waxed cold. Mental illness is at an all-time high, suicide rates has increased, and the lives of the young are being taken by the wicked one at a faster rate. There seems to be no security anywhere. No place of safety. The justice system is failing the innocent, and the ones who promise to 'serve and protect' are neglecting their oath to the people. The principalities of evil seem to have a hold on all of society.

But there is a 'people'. There is a generation and race of individuals that dwell in the land, who possess the power to make change and impact. To shine light and hope for the broken hearted. To extend healing and wholeness to the mentally disturbed. The hope of Life and the revelation of THE WAY to the one who think death is the only way. The grace and power to snatch the young soul from the grips of sin and death, and the VOICE to advocate God's Justice and vindication to the oppressed and less fortunate. These people are the church of Christ!

God is doing something mighty. The restoration of His GREAT Glory upon the church. This is why God is calling us to align ourselves. To sanctify ourselves. He desires to meet with His people and manifest His shekinah even amid His assemblies. God want to be seen amid His church. God want the world to know that there is a God in the camp of His people. The LORD desires to make the places where His people are gathered, places of healing and restoration. Places of hope and encouragement. Places where Death is exchange for salvation and life in Jesus! God desire to reveal His glory through the church! This is the purpose of this book. The purpose to communicate to you that mind of God concerning His church. His purpose regarding advancing His Kingdom and revealing His glory. The glory He committed to His church through His son. This is the Glory of God.

CHAPTER ONE

A Call to Sanctification

I would not be telling you the truth if I were to tell you that the making of this book happened through a sudden revelation. No, but through a series of revelations that God was revealing to me since I was 16 years old. This was around the time when I was in a season, where God was dealing with me profoundly about his church. The hand of God was indeed upon me. God was dealing with me in visions and dreams concerning the 'Glory' that God wants the church to walk in, the power that God desires to manifest once again through His church. Where signs and wonders would become the norm again within the church, while the gospel is being preached. The restoration of boldness, confidence, faith, and power that the first century church walked in. I'm talking about the same power the church walked in that we read about in the book of acts that were recorded by the skilled physician Luke.

Yes, the glory and the power that Christ committed unto the church, through the outpouring of the Spirit, is on the rise. God is making a call throughout the assemblies (churches) to allow His glory to return, because the days are dark and the winning of souls to Christ is imminent. The harvest is still great, and the Lord is calling laborers into the vineyard (Matthew 9:35-38). This Is a time to come out from among any entanglement of sin. Anything that is binding or hindering you from increasing in God. It's time to lose it and untie it from your life. God is calling the church to sanctification. Time is growing thin for some of His people. He is calling you right now! You have an assignment that He has for you to do. The call of God is on you. That call is to show forth his glory.

The Apostle Peter writes it this way, "But you are not like that, for you are a chosen people. You are royal priests, a holy nation, God's very own possession. As a result, you can show others the goodness of God, for he called you out of the darkness into his wonderful light." (1 peter 2:9). We, as believers, are called to live a life that shows His glory (promise) to others. Our life should show to a dying world the power of God. You know for yourself what you used to do before you meet Christ. However, now that you're in Christ, you have tasted and experienced the transforming power of God. How He brought you out of "darkness" into His marvelous light. We are called to walk a life that shows His glory and power. Therefore, God is calling His people to live a more sanctified life.

"I brought you out of Egypt, to bring you unto myself."

(Exodus 19:4)

For 430 years, the Hebrews were in Egypt as slaves and in bondage. A wicked pharaoh emerged and imposed his rule on God's holy people, depriving them of their freedom. According to Exodus, this pharaoh was ignorant of who Joseph was. (Exodus 1:8). Israel's descendants multiplied and prospered in the land of Goshen. The pharaoh saw this and became intimidated, saying, "Behold, the people of the children of Israel are more and mightier than we; come on, let us deal wisely with them; lest they multiply, and it comes to pass, that when there falls out any war, they join also unto our enemies, and fight against us and so get them up out the land (Exodus 1:9-10). Inside of the heart and imagination of the pharaoh became continuously evil towards the Israelites. Therefore, he dealt shrewdly with them. Throughout their time in slavery, the Hebrews cried out to the Lord to deliver them (Exodus 3:9), and so the Lord raised Moses to deliver them out of Egypt. By an outstretched hand from the Almighty God, He judged the kingdom of Pharoah by smiting all of Egypt with His wonders. With a strong and outstretched hand, He brought the children of Israel out of bondage and oppression. Where He brought them unto Sanai, where He showed them His glory and gave them His word. To consecrate them and sanctify them. His intention was for them to become a treasured possession and a holy nation unto Him.

By the Spirit of God and the testimony of our Christ, the same story Israel has pertaining to being in bondage, the church possesses it as well. The same 'right' and 'testimony' they have concerning being God's holy nation and kingdom (in the visible world), we, the church, possess this as well. However, the church holds the legalistic document of being a "spiritual" inheritance of God, purchased by the blood of Jesus Christ. While the nation of Israel holds the legalistic document of being the 'physical' or natural inheritance of God. But both portray God's glory in a sense. But only through the Christ (the Messiah) can both become one!

However, I digress. We, the people of God, were in a state of Egypt as well. When we were living luxuriously in our sins. We were in bondage to sin and the prince of this world. The Apostle Paul declares we walked according to the course of this world, and according to the prince of the power of the air. The spirit that now works in the children of disobedience, used to operate in us (Ephesians 2:2). We were indeed slaves to sin. But we can thank God that when our sins trapped and enslaved us, He sent someone like Moses to us. A deliverer who is Jesus, the CHRIST OF Nazareth. He purchased us with His blood and made us kings and priests unto God. Just like God used Moses to bring Egypt unto Him (as a mediator), so the Lord used His Son Jesus to bring us to Himself.

> "Unto him that loved us and washed us from our sins in his own blood, 6 And hath made us kings and priests unto God and his Father; to him be glory and dominion for ever and ever. Amen. (Revelations 1:5b-6)

> "for thou wast slain, and hast redeemed us to God by thy blood out of every kindred, and tongue, and people, and nation;" (Revelations 5:9b)

> " For there is one God, and one mediator between God and men, the man Christ Jesus;" (1 timothy 2:5)

> "And for this cause he (Jesus the Christ) is the mediator of the New Testament, that by means of death, for the redemption of the transgressions that were under the first testament, they which are called might receive the promise of eternal inheritance." (Hebrews 9:15)

Grace For Grace

When God brought the children of Israel out of Egypt and into the mountain of Sanai, He called Moses up to the Mountain. The Lord gave Moses words to say to the house of Israel. First reminding them to look back and behold how He delivered them out of Egypt. How He bored them on eagle wings out of the land of bondage and brought them to himself. Now the Lord's tone switches. His mind shifts from the past to the present. There was a call to action. He was now speaking to Israel. He was now calling them to respond to His "Grace." To not just respond to what He just did, but to the reason He did what He did. In Exodus 19:5, the Bible mentions that if you truly obey my voice and uphold my covenant, you will be a unique treasure to me, surpassing all others. God was calling Israel into His grace. By accepting His covenant that He was about to give to them, and by them obeying His commandments. The Grace to be a peculiar treasure to Him above all people on the earth. Yes, a holy nation. This is what the Grace of God called them into. To be a person plucked out to be used by Him. to shine His glory to the other nations. This was the grace He was calling them into. For them to truly become a holy and royal priesthood. To be above all the nations. To be priests before God, their savior (Isaiah 61:6).

Moses was the mediator between God and the children of Israel. God communicated to Moses the divine Law upon Mt. Sanai. The Ten Commandments. These are the commandments that contain God's universal law, and these commandments contain His grace. The grace to be a person called by Him. Only when the people "respond" to His grace by obeying His voice and keeping the covenant would they walk in that grace. It was through Moses, the lawgiver they got the testimony to receive this, Grace.

Roughly 1396 years after Moses, the word itself became flesh. The covenant that contains the very Grace decided to clothe himself in the likeness of sinful flesh. He concluded it was fitting for Him to be born of a virgin who was betrothed to a righteous man from the line of David. So, His coming could fulfill scriptures (Isaiah 11:1). To be born in Bethlehem, the very city of David, and to be born in a manger (a feeding trough for the farm animals). Jesus of Nazareth is His name. He is that Grace that John testified about in the gospel of John (John 1:16). He is the Light that shines in the darkness, and the darkness cannot overcome it. The one who came to His own but His own did not receive Him. The very people who stated that Moses was their mediator and law giver rejected the very law itself. He is the WORD OF GOD. He is the very "Grace" that is freely given from God to all who accept Him. All that enter covenant with God through Him.

Therefore, John says, "and all of his fullness have all we received and grace for grace." (John 1:16). Jesus, the word of God. The very testimony and covenant of God extended to them (And us) a continuous flow of God's grace and power. What is this "grace and power"? Exodus 19 says, "A peculiar people and treasure unto me." John says, "The power to become the sons of God." (John 1:12). This is the Grace offered to us. He offered it first to Israel, calling them His firstborn son because he entered a covenant with them first (Exodus 4:22). Now He offers it to the world. Through His Son Jesus. He offered it to Israel by giving them His covenant through Moses. Now He offers it to the world through the word itself, Jesus the Christ, and to all who believe in Him accept the "Grace". Moses was the mediator between God and Israel. Jesus is the mediator between God and humanity. Only in Him do we, the church, have the grace (the power) to keep becoming sons of God. The "peculiar people and treasure" to Him.

The Power To Become.

It is fitting to say that the children of Israel went wayward like rebellious children many times. Throughout the bible (old and New Testament), we read stories and testimonies regarding their rebellion. Yet, God, each time would pursue them because He loved them. But you see, God knew this. He knew that human flesh alone could not keep the law. He knew this. Before He even laid the foundations of the universe and spoke everything into existence, He knew. Before He shaped and fashioned the Earth from molten rocks in space, He knew this. He knew that the children of Israel would break His covenant. He knew it was impossible for man in their humanity to keep the covenant. Works alone could not save them. The blood from bulls, goats, and sheep yearly did not suffice the yearly sin offerings for the people. These sacraments alone could not secure the individual soul a place to receive His "Grace." No, they could not. Since God knew this, He already prepared and offered His own sacrifice. Before He laid the foundations of the universe and spoke everything into existence. Before He shaped and fashioned the earth from molten rocks, He was already prepared and sacrificed as the ultimate sin offering. The bible says, "He was the Lamb slain since the foundation of the world." (Revelation 13:8).

Although Israel, His firstborn, broke the covenant, all was not lost. The covenant indeed was a shadow of things to come. It was pointing to the LIVING AND EVERLASTING COVANANT. The very Covenant that'll never fail. What is this covenant? You may ask. It is Jesus, the Son of God. He is the Word of God. So, the covenant is also still good and alive, because the covenant is a person. If the covenant is still good, then the "Grace" in it is still good and being offered by God. The Grace to "become" sons of God. In this Covenant, we do not have to sacrifice animals or perform religious sacraments to receive the "Grace." The only response that is required is "Faith" in Christ. Believing in and accepting Jesus for who He is. This alone opens the door for the Spirit to dwell in us, and in the Spirit alone abides the seed of the "Grace" to become.

God indeed called Israel His firstborn among the Nations because it was unto them (as fleshly descendants of Abraham) God gave them His covenant. He first extended His grace to them (as a nation). He provided them with His covenant and gave them a promise; "If you obey my voice indeed, and keep my covenant, then you shall be a peculiar treasure unto me above all people; and you shall be unto me a kingdom of priests, and a holy nation." (Exodus 19:5-6). This was only if they kept His covenant, then would they have walked in the sonship. As a peculiar and treasured person. A kingdom of priests and a holy nation. They would have indeed been walking in the "grace."

But the summation of the covenant is in Christ. He is the very word of God. He is the Logos (written word) and the Rhama (utterance and spoken word). Therefore, if the Grace to "become" is found in God's word and covenant by accepting it in your heart; then the "Grace" to become must be in Christ, because He is the word of God (John 1:1, 1:14).

The Spirit of Grace

We talked about how God extended through His covenant His grace; and how His covenant, His word, and His testimony is Jesus alone. He first extended His grace (through His covenant) to Israel, and now through Christ (who is the very word and covenant of God), He extends it to the world. Now, the question is, what is this "Grace"? What is so special about this "Grace"? Why is the power to become sons of God found in "Grace" alone? The answer is that this "Grace" is the gift of God, and the gift of God is the Spirit. The Spirit of God. He is that Spirit of Grace.

We find the grace of the Spirit of Christ in accepting Christ. The Spirit of God is the very power that enabled us to "become" sons of God. The transforming Power of the Spirit transformed our spirit into the likeness of Christ. Understand this truth; Christ is the expressed image of the Father, and we are the expressed image of Christ. Therefore, through the spirit, we are sons of God because of Christ. That is why it is through this Spirit of Grace we are Christ (Romans 8:9).

The Apostle Paul explains more profoundly in Romans

8:12-17 that the Spirit of God, the Spirit of Grace, adopted us as the children of God. The Spirit provides us with the power and grace to "become". What makes it more astounding is that the Spirit witnesses to our spirit. He reassures our spirit about the adoption of sons. He witnesses to our spirit the words, testimony of the covenant. Which is Jesus Christ. Anyone who accepts Christ and His testimony receives the Spirit. They are born again by the Spirit and receive the "Grace" to "become sons of God."

This is the very thing the spirit witness to our spirit; "As many as received him, to them gave the power to become the sons of God. Even to them that believe in his name." (John 1:12), and then He'll say, "you accepted Christ by believing and receiving His testimony. Therefore, I am the evidence. I am the "Grace." That power and legitimization of your right of "becoming" God's son." by the Spirit are we a part of the Family of God. By the Spirit, we are a part of His house.

No longer are we slaves, and no longer are we in Egypt. But we are sons. In the same way, He bore Israel on eagle wings out of bondage to Himself, so did He bring us to Himself by the Spirit. By accepting Christ, we entered His covenant. Therefore, we received the "Grace" to become His sons. But when the Spirit entered those of us who believe. To those of us He indwells, He did not come empty-handed. No, but He brought along with Him spiritual endowments of gifts and graces.

The endowments of priesthood
(Spiritual gifts)

The Apostle Paul declares in Ephesians 2:1-10 that we were all dead because of sin. No life was in us, and we were slaves to the prince of the air. No life was in us, and we were slaves to the prince of the air. We walked according to the course of this world and feasted on our lustful desires. We were brutes. Wildman and woman, carried away by the flesh and the control of sin. There was a complete absence of self-control. We inhabited a behavior that was unfitting of royalty. We were not re-fashioned in the Image of God, which is why this happened. But then Paul says in Ephesians 2:4, "But God…" God, in the richness of His mercy and love, quickened us! How did He quicken us (or make us alive)? Through the "Grace" given unto us through Christ Jesus. The Grace of God is rich and meaningful in its Greek connotation. Grace here in this scripture denotes God's gift, blessing, favor, and kindness. That entailed in God's grace is the fullness of God's life! Through His grace, we are "saved". Through His grace we received His "kindness", and through His grace, we received His "gift". Therefore, God made us alive through His Grace in Christ.

But what brings the Grace of God into the life of a believer? What brings the endowments of the priesthood? It is the Spirit of God. Remember, we stated earlier how the Spirit indwells everyone who believes that Jesus is the Son of God and follows Him. He adopts us as sons of God. As sons of God, we are peculiar people and a treasured nation unto God. We are a royal priesthood, because the Spirit of God entered us, regenerated us, and made us alive through the grace of God. The Grace of God is rich and bountiful, and because it gets the gift, the blessing, and favor of God; the Grace of God imparted into every believer the endowments of priesthood, and those endowments are the gifts of the Spirit.

The spiritual gifts

The "gift" given to all believers is the Spirit of God. Through the Grace of Christ, we have been given a gift. The Spirit indeed is the "gift" that administered "gifts" to the people of God. Within every believer, the Spirit of God (the gift) imparted gifts. Apostle Paul talks about this in 1 Corinthians 12.

> *"Now there are diversities of gifts, but the same Spirit. There are differences between administrations, but the same Lord. And there are diversities of operations, but it is the same God which worketh." (1 Corinthians 12:4-6)*

"The same Spirit, but diversities of gifts!" Every believer receives gifts from the Spirit. There are differences in administrations, but the same Lord. The Spirit of God, the gift of God, made us alive through God's bountiful grace! He made us one body, one living organism in our Lord Jesus Christ; and through the Grace of God, imparted into the heart of every believer these supernatural gifts to show the world the love, power, and grace of God to every creature in the earth. He made us alive and empowered us through these supernatural gifts and graces to manifest (through many manifestations) the richness of God's life in Christ.

This is the endowment of priesthood, and we are so impacted by these supernatural gifts, grace, and Power, because of the gift; Now that we know such a measure this "Grace" entails, what are we going to do to walk in it?

The revelation

From the time of Moses passing down the Ten Commandments to Israel, to the emergence of Christ from the "shadows of things to come" in the New Testament; there is a prophetic message to the church. God descended upon Mt. Sanai in the similitude of His glory and spoke to the children of Israel. He meets with them. Although they could not stand to hear His voice, Moses could. So, God used Moses to be the mediator between them and God. Moses handed them the Ten Commandments and spoke a word of endearment from the Father to them, "If you'll obey my voice and keep my covenant, then you shall be a peculiar treasure unto me above all people! And you shall be unto me a kingdom of priests, and a holy nation." (Exodus 19:5-6).

God manifested His glory to Israel. He extended to them an invitation to receive His "Grace". The grace to become His "sons" and walk as a kingdom of priests and a holy nation. Where He Manifest His glory, Power, and Name to them and through them so the entire world could seek! God desired to not only rest on Mt. Sanai, but He wanted to "rest" on them!

This is the call to the assemblies. This is the call to the bride of Christ here in America. Jesus, the word of God and everlasting covenant, contains the Grace we all received in our hearts to "become" sons of God! All born-again believers possess the Grace, because the Spirit of Christ lives in them! He is the Grace to "become"! Also in the Grace, He distributed gifts. He distributed God's blessing, favor, power, and ability! He imparted to every believer His glory! But you see, He did not just do this so we could just sit around and relax. He did not impact us with these gifts, so we could hide, fall away, and become like the culture. No! But so, we could walk in them, and allow the Spirit to demonstrate God's power in many ways and preach the gospel. Now is the time to rise and shine. It's time to get up. It's time to wake up from our slumber. Hear the words of the Lord through Apostle Paul;

> "And that, knowing the time, that now it is high time to awake out of sleep; for now, is our salvation nearer than when we believed." Romans: 13:11)

Then he proceeds to say in verse 12,

> "The night is far spent; the day is at hand; let us therefore cast off the works of darkness and let us put on the armor of light!"

The time has come. The time is now. The world is growing increasingly dark, and many assemblies (congregations, denominations) are falling by the wayside. The LORD is calling His people to Arise. The Remnant that remains. The Lord is calling for us to arise and wash our garments. To sanctify ourselves, for the day of our beautification has arisen.

> *"AWAKE, awake; put on thy strength O Zion; Put on thy beautiful garments, O' Jerusalem, the holy city."*

(Isaiah 52:1)

The Lord is beseeching us to put on our garments of righteousness and light. For thus saith the Lord;

"For the time is drawing short, and

My words will begin to unravel quickly.

I want my people to be prepared and to be positioned.

For I desire to come down upon the Mount of the

Assembly of my church and rest upon them."

-Words of the Father

Awake, awake O Zion. For the Lord desires to reveal His Glory amongst His people, and He wants every one of us to be apart and be a part of His workmanship.

CHAPTER TWO

The Days of Joel

Somewhere between 8-9 years ago, the church I used to belong to choose me to pray in a worship service. The name of the church was called St. Paul Church of Christ disciples of Christ. The church was known as the church sitting on the "hill" because of its elevated location in the town where I grew up. One Sunday, in a youth service, I was chosen to do the morning prayer. Now this was not my first time praying in a church service. Normally, during choir rehearsal, they would choose who would pray, and every night when I was chosen, I would seek God to sanctify me for His service to pray the next morning. I have always been a person where when I am called to handle God's business, I want it to be Him working through me for the building up of His Name and glory. Not my own.

So, here I go the following morning during the service. It was time for prayer. Nervous and shaking inwardly, I approach the podium on the floor. I say an inward prayer asking the Lord to have His way. I open my mouth, and before I knew it, the Spirit of God immersed me in His power and took control. It was no longer me praying, but the Spirit praying through me. While praying, I heard the Spirit of the Lord speak through me, saying, "For the glory of the Lord shall return to the House of God." As a 16-year-old teenager, in my humanity, I did not know that God was preparing and equipping me for this book. For this ministry. To declare to the assemblies and the corporate body of Christ regarding what space and time the church is approaching, on God's prophetic timetable.

We have been for some time in the "END TIME HARVEST." Since the day of Pentecost, we have been on such days. The days where God is extending salvation to the masses and the fields of the Lord are ready to be harvested. But as Jesus declared in Matthew, "Pray that the Lord of the harvest sends forth laborers into his harvest." God is just now looking for laborers to go forth and harvest the multitude of souls unto Him. The words God spoke to Isaiah is ringing in my ears;

"Whom shall I send, and who will go for us?" (Isaiah 6:8 AMP)

Too often, we quote this scripture as an excuse to be passive regarding going out into the vineyard;

"But understand this; On the last day's terrible times will come. For men will be lovers of themselves, lovers of money, boastful, abusive, disobedient to their parents, ungrateful, unholy, unloving, unforgiving, slanderous, without self-control, without love of good.. having godliness but denying the power." Timothy 3:1-7)

Also, most of us try to use the words of Jesus to justify our action of being passive when it concerns evangelizing out in the world;

"Because of the increase of wickedness, the love of most will grow cold," (Matthew 24:12 NIV)

We try to use these scriptures to justify our thoughts and statements such as, "the bible said the world will become worse. So, what can you do?" There seems to be no more zeal or ferventness in many believers in America.

Some of us try to push the Job on the pastor, the minister, the Apostle, the Prophet, the evangelist, the teacher, and the bishop. We try to say, "It's their job to spread the word and witness and bring souls into the Kingdom." This is not true. We are in the days of Joel. The Spirit of God in the Old Testament only rested on kings, priests, and prophets. But now Jesus has made it possible where the Spirit dwells with and in all believers. The prophet Joel saw these years before the "year of God's favor." The time where God will give "Grace for Grace" (the continues flow of God's grace/power) to all that believe in His Son. In Joel 2:28-32, the prophet saw something that was wondrous. A day of Joel is where God will take His Spirit and freely pour it out on everyone. No matter your social class or age. The day of Joel is a day where the Lord gives His Spirit freely, without distinction. We are in those days. The days of Joel.

God is calling every believer to walk out this prophecy. To walk in the power of the Spirit. The day we accepted Christ was the very day Christ indwelled us by His Spirit. There is another level of Power we all are called to. That level and authority of priests of God, and a holy nation. To show forth His praises and glory; and the first initiative in entering this glory is through the regenerative work of the Holy Spirit, which is His baptism.

The Baptism of the Spirit

The day we accepted Christ into our hearts and repented of our sins, the Spirit of Christ entered our hearts. Any man or woman who makes that life-changing decision, of turning away from sin and turning towards Jesus, the Spirit of God indwells them. He gives them a new heart. A regenerated one. See, this is the first work of the Holy Spirit as He entered the heart of the believer. He regenerates the heart into salvation. He gives the believer a clean heart. A heart of flesh (for God, obedience) and not of stone (rebellion). The prophet Ezekiel prophesied this;

> *"A New heart also I will give you, and a new spirit will I put within you. And I will take away the stony heart out of your flesh, and I will give you a heart of flesh." (Ezekiel 36:26)*

The prophet Ezekiel saw the time when the Lord would make it possible for the Spirit to regenerate the heart. Look at this, the prophet declares in the verses above 26;

> *"Then I will sprinkle clean water upon you, and ye shall be clean. From all your filthiness and all your idols, I will cleanse you." (Ezekiel 36:25)*

The Lord reveals an imagery of baptism to Ezekiel. A purification ritual accompanies the renewal and regeneration of the heart. This is the true meaning of baptism. It is a purification ritual. The Lord speaks through the prophet that He was going to take His people (Israel) through a purification ritual by "sprinkling" or baptizing them in water. Through this, He will cleanse them; and the cleansing causes a new regenerated heart.

See, this shows one of the first works of the Spirit in a believer's life when it concerns salvation. The baptism where He cleanses us and regenerates us into sons. Through this work of salvation, He adopts us into becoming sons of God. He puts the seal of God on our hearts through our open confession that Jesus is Lord and our faith that God raised Him from the dead.

> *"If you openly declare that Jesus is Lord and believe in your heart that God raised Him from the dead, you will be saved."(Romans 10:9)*

By putting one's trust in the resurrected savior, the Spirit enters His or her heart and regenerates it into a heart of righteousness. See, the Holy Spirit is the baptized. He is the one who grants us the authority through His baptism to become a part of Christ's body. The Apostle Paul talks about this baptism in 1 Corinthians 12:13;

> *"Some of us are Jews, some are gentiles, some are slaves, and some are free. But one Spirit has baptized us into one body, and we all share the same Spirit."* (1 Corinthians 12:13)

The Spirit has baptized every believer (not by water alone) into Christ. It's through the Spirit we are connected as one! On the day, hour, minute, and second when we said "yes" to the call to repentance and acceptance of salvation in Christ through the preached gospel, the Spirit entered us and imparted a regenerated heart into us. At that moment, we were baptized into Christ Jesus. Everything God does is already a completed work. God never does a partial work, but He always does a completed work. Therefore, the Work of the Spirit regeneration is of salvation and life, and we know that salvation is a completed work.

"You Must be born again"

There was a man named Nicodemus. He was a pharisee, a Jewish leader who was very well respected. One day he decided to approach Jesus at night to talk to him secretly. The first thing Nicodemus says to Jesus is, "Rabbi, we know that you are a teacher that comes from God. For no man can do these miracles that thou doest, except God be with him." (John 3:1-2). Nicodemus acknowledge Jesus to be a teacher, and to be legit because of the Miracles. The Mirales was the signature of God on Jesus testimony (John 5:36). Now, on hearing this Jesus saw it to be an opportunity to teach Nicodemus the mysteries of God's Kingdom, and one of that Mystery in this message found in chapter 3 is the "rebirth through the Holy Spirit."

Jesus reply to Nicodemus was sharp and straight to the point; "Verily, Verily, I say unto you, except a man be born again, he cannot see the Kingdom of God." (John 3:3). Yes indeed, no man can see (or experience) the Kingdom of God, unless He is born again. No, not born again through natural birth. No, Jesus is not talking about reincarnation: Living many lives and being reborn repeatedly. Heaven do not have such a caste system. Nicodemus thought Jesus was referring to being born again through Natural birth. Jesus had to then explain to Nicodemus;

"Verly, Verily, I say to you; Except a man be born of water and of the Spirit, he cannot enter into the kingdom of God." (John 3:5)

Jesus had to explain to Nicodemus this is spiritual. Nothing that is of this world can bring about this rebirth. Only the Spirit of God can regenerate. See, the writer John records Jesus saying, "Being born of water and of the Spirit." Some denomination teach that this is physical water baptism. It is true that the language Christ is using is synonymous to baptism, but the Spirit in Himself carries the components and working of Water. The Spirit Himself cleanses and purifies the same way water do. It's possible

Jesus was referring to physical birth as well (water). As Nicodemus thought he was referring to being born again physically, and Jesus response was to correct Nicodemus perception. But you see, Jesus was speaking as the Messiah to Nicodemus. He was speaking as the Son of God. Jesus was letting Nicodemus know that I am more then a "teacher". I am the one who was promised by the prophets to bring about the cleansing of the heart. This is also why Jesus says, "being born of water and of the Spirit".

The Greek usage of this scripture is, "even of the Spirit." Jesus was plainly communicating to Nicodemus that the same way water purifies and cleanses, "even so" the Spirit. Jesus was saying to Nicodemus that he must be regenerated and cleansed. Jesus was referring to being born again by the Spirit in this way. Being baptized this way. Such concept that Jesus was speaking to Nicodemus should not had been a surpirse to him. This is why when Nicodemus said, "how can this be?" Jesus then says to Nicodemus, "you are Israel teacher, and you don't understands these things?" Nicodemus were famliar with what the prophet Ezekiel says "and I will give you a new heart" and "I will sprinkle clean water over you and clean you from all your filthiness" (Ezekiel 35:25-26). Therefore, this is the "baptism", being born again and regenerated by the Spirit.

To be born again one must be regenerated by the Spirit. One must be born anew. The same way the world was made anew by the flood of Noah and being baptized by the waters thereof. The same way the children of Israel was baptized into the law of Moses by crossing the red sea. The same way John the Baptist followers was baptized into his preaching of repentance by dipping into the Jordan river. Is the same way we are baptized unto Christ and into the kingdom by the baptism of the Spirit through His regeneration.

> "And that water is a picture of baptism, which now saves you, not by removing dirt from your body, but as a response

to God from a clean conscience. It is effective because of the resurrection of Jesus Christ." (1 peter 3:21 NLT)

"Moreover, brethren, I would not that ye should be ignorant, how that all our fathers were under the cloud, and all passed through the sea; and were all baptized unto Moses in the cloud and in the sea;" (1 Corinthians 10:2 KJV)

The Holy Ghost and Fire

Out In the wilderness of Judea, the word of God comes to a man by the name of John. The gospel writer Luke records in chapter 3, verses 1-2 the current gentile rulers who were placed over areas in the land of Judah. The Jews were in a time of oppression from Rome. They were in the time that God prophesied would come in Daniel's 70 weeks prophecy (Daniel 9). According to God's prophetic calendar, Israel was in the middle of the 70-week prophecy, where the Messiah should come. All Israel was expecting for Him to come. As the times they were currently in pointed to His coming. God, the sovereign King over the universe, now was about to intercept into the history of man. While the kings and rulers of the world were being born and ruling, the universal king is about to appear to the world. God is now implementing His divine and eternal plan of salvation into the history of man. Jesus of Nazareth, the Messiah, His ministry was about to begin.

Therefore, the word of God comes to John. John was the prophesied "forerunner" of the Christ. The prophet Isaiah prophesied.

> "He is a voice shouting in the wilderness. Prepare the way of the Lord's coming! Clear the road for him! The valleys will be filled, and the mountains and hills made level. The curves will be straightened, and the rough places made smooth. And then all people will see the salvation sent from God." (Isaiah 40:3-5)

This John was baptizing in the Jordan River, preaching the good news regarding repentance of remissions of sins. Crowds from the surrounding areas came out to see John.

To hear this great message of repentance and preparation of the 'Lords' visitation. While he was preaching and baptizing, the crowds began to wonder whether John was the Massiah. The people of Israel were expecting Him to come soon, on account of the signs of the present age, oppression, and ancient prophecies pointed to such a time. John answered their questions and wanderings with,

> "I baptize you with water, but someone is coming soon who is greater than I am- so much greater that I'm not even worthy to be his slave and untie the straps of his sandals. He will baptize you with the Holy Spirit and with Fire." (Luke 3:16)

John makes a major distinction between his baptism and the Massiah. John states that His baptism was with water. John's baptism with water symbolizes the washing away of sins. His baptism followed his message of repentance and reformation of the heart. But Christ's baptism, according to John, would be of the "Holy Spirit and Fire. John declares that the baptism of Christ will baptise with is with the Spirit's power to do God's will. That Christ will grant His followers (those that believe in Him), the supernatural "grace" to do the work of the Lord as a 'sanctified people'. To be His empowered witnesses. This is the baptism that every believer is baptized with. Christ baptized us with the Spirit. The baptism we who are in Christ is baptized with the Holy Ghost and even fire.

Now, let us consider "and fire". Fire in the scriptures symbolizes purification. For example, Numbers 31:23 says, "And anything else that can withstand fire must be put through the fire, and then it will be clean; and it shall be purified with the water of purification. But all that cannot endure fire you shall put through the water" (Numbers 31:23, NIV). Or Malachi 3:2, "But who can endure the day of his coming? Who can stand it when he appears? For he will be like a refiner's fire or a launderer's soap." (Malachi 3:2 NIV). In retrospect to it referring to God's judgement, many scriptures refer to God's wrath and judgement as that of fire (Just like Malachi 3:2 talking about the day of his coming). Other scriptures such as Jeremiah 4:4 which says, "Circumcise yourselves to the LORD and remove the foreskins of your heart, men of Judah and inhabitants of Jerusalem, or else my wrath will go forth like fire and burn with none to quench it, because of the evil of your deeds." (Jeremiah 4:4). Isaiah 66:15 says, "For behold, the LORD will come in fire and His chariots like the whirlwind, to render His anger with fury, and His rebuke with flames of fire."

Keeping those two things in mind, I want to first focus on the symbolism of purification. Remember I spoke about how "being born again," and the Spirit's work of "regeneration" is a spiritual purification ritual. The Spirit sprinkled us and immersed us in God's water. Not only water, but fire. God, through His Spirit and faith in Christ, purified us and consecrated us. He separated us unto Himself. This is why after John mentions, "Holy Ghost and fire," He continues by stating in verse 17, "then he will clean up the threshing floor, gathering the wheat into His born." That Christ baptizes us with the Spirit and fire of purification. To sanctify us unto Him, and why does He sanctify us unto Himself? He does it for the reason of the other meaning and function of symbolism of fire, and that is "Judgement."

Judgement; the gospel of Christ

John the Baptist, while preaching in the wilderness and making His statement of Christ's baptism, begins to explain the work of Christ's ministry and baptism. He makes this explanation of course in verse 17. "His winnowing fork is in his hand to clear his threshing floor and to gather the wheat into his barn, but he will burn up the chaff with unquenchable fire." (Luke 3:17) John was declaring that Christ was coming not only to baptize with fire of purification but to also bring judgement. That the very work and ministry of Christ (even today) is judgment. It is fire. The ministry and testimony Christ carried were Judgement in itself, and since He is the word of God, the eternal fate of the hearer is in what they decide to do with it once hearing it. To those who receive Him, He purifies and casts into His barn. But to them that refuse, He burns with unquenchable fire. As people of God, we are called to carry out this ministry. We are called to carry out this work of judgement.

"This is Judgement work"

I remember many of the older saints in the community where I was raised, when admonishing the younger ministers they would say, "You are doing Judgement work." What they were saying was that being a minister of the gospel is the very judgement work of God. But to everyone in the body of Christ, to all of God's people, we are all called to do such a work. We are all called to be ministers of the LORD. What I mean is witnesses to the good news. We are all called to do "Judgement work." The Apostle Paul declares that we are all called to be "ministers of reconciliation." (2 Corinthians 5:18). That God reconciled us unto

Himself and gave us all the ministry of reconciliation.

This is the called to the body of Christ in this hour. To walk in this "Judgement work", and to walk in the ministry of reconciliation. This is the "fire" John the Baptist's reference to Jesus' ministry. That Jesus will baptize with the Holy Ghost and fire. I previously stated how fire biblically symbolized purification, and how he purified us and sanctified us unto Christ. For a "specific" work. Now, I want to address that work. The work of Fire. The work of Judgement.

Now, to better lay this work and ministry of Christ call us to this judgement work. We must first point out the relationship between the Holy Spirit and Christ's ministry. The ministry that God committed to Christ (as the Massiah), was empowered by the Spirit. The ministry of Christ is compacted with the Spirit. The very work of Christ was charged by the Spirit Himself. We see this when Christ was baptized. In Luke 3:21-22, The Spirit descended upon Him after He was baptized. To anoint Him for the work of the ministry God ordained. The power and fire of the Spirit engulfed the very work Christ was sent to do.

The very ministry of our Christ was judgement work indeed because the ministry of Christ entails the very work of the Holy Spirit, who brings God's judgement. That Judgement is the testimony of Christ.

"The Judgement in denying the son"

John the Baptist, in our focus scripture, clearly defines the judgment work Christ will carry out. That the very testimony He carries also entails judgment. John the Baptist declares in Luke 3:17, "He is ready to separate the chaff from the wheat with His winnowing fork, He will clean up the threshing area, gathering the wheat into His barn but burning the chaff with never-ending fire." John the Baptist was not only referencing Jesus as being the "great separator" but that He is also the Judge. The very work, ministry, and testimony He carries will also usher in judgment against "weeds" and "wheat" (Matthew 13:24-30). But what is the testimony that Jesus carried that ushered in God's kingdom? It is the testimony of Himself.

"The testimony of the son"

In John chapter five, Jesus heals a man at the pool of Bethesda on the sabbath day. The man sitting at the pool had been lying there for thirty-eight years. The man and the other people who were lame, crippled, blind, withered or any other ailment came to the pool looking for some hope of salvation from their illness. In your King James Bible verse four says, "For an angel went down at a certain season into the pool and troubled the water: whosoever then first after the troubling of the water stepped in was made whole of whatsoever disease he had." Some Bibles do not include or have a verse four. If you look at most other modern translations such as NIV (New International Version) or the NLT (New Living Translation), you'll see it skips to verse 5. The reason is that the earliest manuscripts did not contain this section of the verse. Therefore, we do not know for sure if an angel came down to trouble the water, but we know Christ came, the one who possesses the living water meets the man.

Christ, the word of God, the son of God, came to this broken man and healed him. A man in despair and in the spirit of hopelessness. Christ healed Him. Christ appeared to man as eternal hope. Now, after Jesus healed Him, the religious leaders desired to kill Him. But Jesus gives a defense of His work and His testimony. He gives a defense of His deity. Jesus' defense is that God exalted the Son and committed unto Him judgment; "so that all may honor the Son, as they honor the Father." And "anyone who does not honor the son, does not honor the Father who sent Him!" (John 5:23). Jesus' testimony of His deity and His work is truly the work of judgment.

The decision of a soul on what it does with it upon hearing it determines its destiny in eternity. The testimony of Christ is indeed judgment work.

The judgment of the testimony of Christ is life or death. Jesus says, "The hour is coming where the dead will hear the voice of the son of God, and those who hear will live." He continues, "For as the Father has life in Himself, so He granted it to the Son because He Is the son of man." (John 5:25-26). Therefore, He has given Him the power to execute Judgement. The judgment of the testimony of Christ is life or death. Therefore, the gospel is judgment work. So, Christ baptizes with the Holy Ghost and fire; the authority to declare judgment (His testimony).

"He will testify of me"

I'm not speaking about the Judgement where we "condemned" folks to hell. I'm not talking about the judgment where we act as "executioners". Standing outside of abortion clinics with signs of "abortion is murder" is not the judgment work the Spirit partakes or carries. No, this fire is of "conviction". I've learned that there is a difference between conviction and condemnation. The work of conviction of the Holy Spirit is all in the proclamation and testimony of Jesus. That is why in John 15:26, He says, "When the advocate comes, the Spirit of truth, He will testify about me." And "When He comes (The Spirit of truth) He will convict (to prove, rebuke, expose, to bring to light) the world of its sin, and of God's righteousness, and the coming judgment. (John 16:8-11). Conviction through the testimony of Christ exposes darkness to bring the individual to the light. Therefore, the work of the Holy Spirit exposes sin in a person's life, through the testimony of Christ, only to bring them to Him to be made complete in God's righteousness.

Jesus declares in John 16:10, "Righteousness is available because I (Jesus) go to the Father, and you will see me no more." Jesus' work, that He did while here on the earth, made it possible and God's righteousness accessible through faith in Him. But man loves wickedness instead of righteousness, and because Christ's work exposed sin and made righteousness accessible, the judgment is now this:

"God's light came into the world, but people loved darkness more than light, for their actions are evil." (John 3:19). The light (truth) of God shines through the testimony of who Christ is. But the judgment is against those who refuse. Also, the judgment is working for those who believe, by granting life eternal. Conviction of the Spirit once again exposes darkness to bring one to the light. While condemnation condemns and provides no grace to escape, or no instructions to get out from under the damnation. Therefore, Christ says;

"I have not come to condemn the world but to save the world through Him." (John 3:17)

"Witnesses of the good news"

Therefore, as the Apostle Paul declares in Ephesians 5:8 that we should "Live as people of light". Why? Because we possess the Light of Life; and what is the Light of Life? Jesus declares in John 8:12, "I am the Light of the world. If you follow me, you won't walk in darkness, because you'll have the light of life." Jesus is the Light of Life. He is the divine illumination of what true life is. Jesus is also the "word." The "word" is truth. Therefore, the word, the testimony of Christ, reveals the True Light to all mankind. It reveals and imparts eternal life to all who receive it. The Light of Life. This is Judgement work.

We as the people of God, the body of Christ, carry the light. We carry the "word" and "truth" of God. That is why, as witnesses, we are called to reveal and proclaim this Light. People of God, we are called to walk in the fire of God. We are called to walk In Christ's work of judgment. Christ is at the right hand of the Father and left us with His Spirit (the Spirit of "truth") to testify of Him. To show the world the Light of life.

Ministers of Fire

The usage and understanding of the word fire in Greek from the biblical stance is that it's used figuratively. In scripture, people interpret fire as an element that has the power to transform everything it comes into contact with, bringing it into Light and likeness with itself. See, God's Spirit enlightens and, as mentioned before, purifies. The Spirit in every believer enlightens us in the word of God. He enlightens our understanding regarding the faith, enabling us to be increasingly conformed to the likeness of Christ. This is important because as this increases the sweetness of our experience in Christ, it creates more boldness to walk in this Fire. To display it. To carry it wherever we go. That in understanding the importance of allowing the Holy Spirit to take preeminence in us, we'll walk in our purpose as the bride of Christ.

As I think more about this, it truly amazes me how the Son of God depended on the supernatural power of the Spirit in carrying out the work of the Father. This shows the key component in walking out the ministry of our Christ; the key component being the Holy Spirit. Jesus walked this earth as the Light and "full of the Holy Spirit and power" (Luke 4:14). Jesus did not depend on His ability or strength. But He allowed the Father to work through Him. This should teach us, who are His disciples, that we cannot do the work Christ committed to us His people without the empowerment of the Spirit. The anointing of the Spirit is what enables our witness to be effective. Therefore, we should seek to carry out this judgment work, declaring the testimony of Christ through the power of the Spirit.

Remember how previously in earlier chapters I mentioned how the moment we accepted Christ, we were baptized unto Him? That the moment we accepted Him by grace through faith, the Spirit entered us and regenerated our hearts. He sealed us until the day of redemption. The Spirit of God granted us the "power to become sons of God." But what if I were to tell you there is "more" than just being a son? That there is a key in fulfilling the work and ministry of Christ committed to all of His church. Connected to the church being baptized in the Holy Ghost on the day of Pentecost, they were "infilled" and empowered.

In Acts chapter one, Jesus commanded His disciples and Apostles to remain in Jerusalem until they received "the promise". The promise is referred to as the "Holy Ghost." You see, the believers had not yet received the Holy Ghost because Jesus had not been glorified yet (John 7:39). Jesus informs His disciples that when the Spirit fills them and baptizes them, they'll receive something. He said they'll receive "power" when He comes upon them. But when the Spirit empowers them, He's going to mobilize them to do a "specific" work. That work is, "to be my witnesses to the world." The Spirit of God indeed filled the disciples and the 120 in the upper room on the day of Pentecost. God's power immersed them. But something I must first talk about in Chapter Two of Acts that was very interesting. To bring the connection to how we, as God's people, ought to walk as God's Ministers of Fire.

"Tongues of fire"

While the disciples (120) were gathered in an upper room chamber, they prayed, fellowshiped, and sang praises to God. Suddenly there was a sound. A roaring and a shaking shook the room they were in. The wind filled the entire house. Now, the scripture here brings out a significant number of theophanies (Manifestation of God's presence), but one stands out particularly. The one I want to focus on for the sake of the message I'm trying to relay to you. As stated in the Bible, they saw flames or tongues of fire settling on each of them. The Holy Spirit filled everyone present, and they began speaking in other languages.

This was an outward manifestation of the glory of God, and the fulfillment of Jesus' promise of sending the comforter, "you shall receive power once the Holy Ghost came upon you" and "You shall be my witnesses." (Acts 1:8). This was the fulfillment to make them His witnesses to all the world! The tongues of flames of fire were the divine ability of the Spirit's power that enabled them to declare, "the wonderful things God had done!" (Acts 2:11) in different known languages. This was the sign; the fulfillment of Jesus' promises to make them His witnesses to all the world. The disciples were now God's ministers of Fire to the world.

The Prophet Joel indeed prophesied this day. When the Lord spoke to Him saying, "I will pour out my spirit upon all flesh", and "your sons and daughters shall prophesy." See, the prophet saw a day when God was going to raise a body and remnant of people born of Fire. Yes, born of Fire (Power, glory, and judgment). That in the last days, the very glory of God will be seen manifested through the ones He has chosen!

"Witnesses in the last days"

During a time when God's judgement is clear, there is a declaration of a remnant who escapes His judgement by calling on His Name. They are the ones who are saved. Not only are they saved, but the LORD gives unto them through His salvation the "grace" of becoming His witnesses. That was what once was only limited to the prophets, kings and priests shown under the old covenant. God now made it available to all who call on His Name, and that is the Power to declare His word and witness.

The prophet Joel speaks so profoundly in this text. He says in verses 30-31, "I will show wonders in the heavens and the earth, blood, fire, and pillars of smoke. The sun shall be turned into darkness, and the moon into blood, before the great and the terrible day of the LORD comes." All are signs and indications of God's judgement, power, glory, and wrath. However, before the great and terrible day of the consummation of His wrath, the prophet says these events shall happen. Can I be the one to say, "It has happened, will continually happen presently, and will happen more in the future?" There's one man whose ministry, life, death, and resurrection started these events. It was Jesus, the Christ of Nazareth.

When Christ was on the cross, it was a time of darkness. Throughout the surrounding hills of the scene of His crucifixion (outside of Jerusalem), you could hear two sounds: the sound of weeping and scoffing. Matthew, Mark, and Luke record that from the sixth to the ninth hour there was darkness over the land as the sun refused to shine (shown by the prophet Joel). As The Son hung on the cross, Judgement was being decreed. On that old rugged cross, Jesus took upon Himself the judgment due to mankind. There on that Cross, He was taking upon Himself the wrath of God. The prophet Isaiah declares it like this;

> *"Surely, He has borne our griefs, and carried our sorrows; yet we did esteem him stricken, smitten of God, and afflicted. But He was wounded for our transgression. He was bruised for our iniquities. The chastisement of our peace was upon him, and with his stripes, we are healed." (Isaiah 53:4-5)*

Through His sacrifice for all humanity, Christ had taken upon himself the judgement of us all, and decreed judgement on the world and the prince thereof (John 12:31-32). When the land grew dark during His crucifixion, it was an announcement of judgment. That sin was once and for all being atoned for, and righteousness is now being made available. Mankind has no excuse for their sins. Mankind now has an escape available. Christ declared in John 12:32; "And I, if I be lifted from the earth, will draw all men unto me." (John 12:32). John continued by saying, "this he said, signifying what death he should die." (John 12:32). That the death of our Christ was the atoning sacrifice to open the door to God's salvation, and the blessed access of becoming God's chosen people, to declare His glory.

Therefore, man has no excuse. The LIGHT of LIFE has made known the way to God. He paved the way to God's righteousness. He made it available. His resurrection was the seal and approval of His sacrifice! His resurrection was the initiation of a new life being made available to all who believe in Him. That they may pass from death to life (John 5:24). That we who believe in Him have died to sin (judgement) and raised to the newness of life by the glory of God (Life eternal; raised into His likeness) (Romans 6). Christ has given salvation to all who call on His name. By Him being approved by God, His work and ministry will go on. He passed the torch. He chose the remnant to go on and testify about Him, and that the signs that accompany Him shall accompany the remnant He chose in these last days.

Is this not what the Prophet Joel prophesied in Verse 32 of chapter 2? Is this not what the Prophet Joel prophesied in Verse 32 of chapter 2? "And it shall come to pass, that whoever calls on the name of the Lord shall be delivered: for deliverance shall be in mount Zion and Jerusalem, as the LORD has said, and in the REMNANT whom the Lord calls." In Christ salvation is made possible (Romans 10:9) by calling on His Name, and in Christ is a remnant of people (the church) He commissioned to carry His light and preach His gospel of salvation! "And in the remnant whom the Lord calls" there lies the way to salvation for the world. The church holds the truth and testimony to bring man to salvation in Christ, and that is the Gospel of Christ!

In these last days, God indeed has raised a remnant. A remnant in Christ. Through their confession of belief, these are the ones who called on His name and were saved. When Peter stood on the balcony of that home, after receiving the promise, he quoted the Joel passage. He was making known to them that what they had witnessed by the disciples speaking in other languages (or in their languages; declaring the wonderful works of God), was the sign. It was the initial manifestation of such a prophecy. The signs in the heavens and earth, fire, blood, and columns of smoke. The power, glory, and judgement of God were here. He made known to them that Jesus the Christ of Nazareth in Himself was the summation of the prophecy. That He was the sign that the last days were here, and the clock is now ticking regarding God's judgement. As He walked among them performing the signs and wonders (Joel 2:30; Acts 2:22). The prophecy states that in these last days, He is the Messiah through whom God promised to save and restore the house of Israel, making it a kingdom of priests and a royal nation. It also promises salvation to the world.

People of God, you are the remanent. You are the ones chosen by Christ to be His ministers of fire. The prophecy of Joel did not just belong to the church found in Acts (first-century church). But it is to you. It belongs to you and your children. He said, "I will pour out my spirit upon you and your children." The priesthood is your heritage in Christ. Therefore, you are His ministers of Fire. The Spirit of God is within you. His ministers of fire are you. The testimony of Christ is something you believe in. You store it in your heart. You walk it and live it. Therefore, it's time to declare it! God desire to back up your work with signs and wonders, as the scriptures have declared, "and these signs shall follow them that believe; in my name shall cast out devils; they shall speak with new tongues.... They shall lay hands on the sick, and they shall recover." (Mark 16:17-18). The glory of God. We are the last day's witnesses, and it's time for the church of God to rise in power and testify about her Christ.

Application of the Matter

People of God, you are that generation of people. The Spirit of God is in you (if you belong to Christ). My job as the messenger of Christ is to tell you that God wants you to know that there are levels of glory in Him. There is such a thing called "infillings". Where the Spirit will fill you and empower you to show forth the glory of God. On the inside of you are the gifts and riches of Christ. The LORD desires to stir that up in you! As a son and a daughter of the King, you are called to witness the wonderful things God has done. He has called you to be a minister of fire.

But you must understand this; the Spirit is the only one who can complete the work through you. Therefore, the power of the Spirit is important. You are called to witness Christ (in fire) to the world. You are called to judgment work. To make known to someone about the LIGHT OF LIFE. You are called to carry His glory, and this glory is witnessing Christ in the Holy Ghost and fire.

"The Infillings"

I know that there are a lot of arguments and disagreements regarding when someone has the Holy Spirit. Some say that the evidence of one having the Holy Ghost is speaking in tongues, and their defense is the book of Acts (2:4), Mark 16:17, and Acts 19:6), and some others believe that the evidence is not in tongues alone, but bearing fruit alone. I chose not to get entangled in debates, but I mentioned this to pave a lead way to the meat of the message.

We know that our place as sons of God is in our faith in Jesus Christ alone. That it is in that alone we are born again. In the previous chapter, I mentioned how through the Spirit alone we are "born again", and "regenerated." I also mentioned how Pentecost was 1) The time when the early church first received the Holy

Spirit. And 2) The fulfillment of Christ's promises to His disciples that He would send the comforter and empower them to be His witnesses to all the nations. Upon entering and infilling them, the Spirit empowered them to declare the "wonderful works of God" supernaturally to the nations. In their languages and tongues. Why am I saying all this? As people of God, we do not have to try to "recreate" Pentecost. We do not have to terry hours upon hours at the altar begging the Father to fill us with the Spirit and looking for a sign to be speaking in tongues, to determine our seal of salvation.

Am I saying that we should not seek to be filled with the Spirit? Not. What I'm saying to you is that the Spirit of God is within you and that your salvation is not in the sign of "speaking in tongues" alone. That is the moment you repented of your sins and accepted Christ into your hearts; The Spirit entered you. He lives in you. See, we can't say we are Christ's if the Spirit is not in us. The Apostle Paul declares:

> *"But ye are not in the flesh, but in the Spirit, if so be that the Spirit of God dwells in you. Now if any man have not the Spirit of Christ, he is none of his." (Romans 8:9)*

People of God, there are levels of glory in God. There are many manifestations of the Spirit's Power that come with the many infillings. See, the Spirit of God is ready and willing to fill every member of your spirit. He is ready and willing to fill every member of the house (the body). He is ready to fill every member in your heart, to show forth the glory of God. As the "Temple" of the Holy Ghost, He is ready to fill your heart daily in unprecedented ways to manifest the glory of God through you.

There is indeed one dwelling, but many "infillings" according to scripture. The Spirit of God desires to fill us up to accomplish the work Christ assigned to us, His people. The disciples in Acts, after being filled with the Holy Ghost in Acts 2, were not "filled" only one time permanently. No, there were multiple incidents of infillings. In Acts 4:23-31, the Apostles and disciples pray. After praying, the place where they were shook, and the bible says each one of them experienced the filling of the Spirit, and spoke the word of God boldly. After hearing the threats and actions of the Pharisees and Sadducees in Jerusalem, the church prayed. God, with His great Power, shook the place and filled it with His Spirit. Filled with boldness, they courageously spoke the word of God! They needed this because they were facing heavy persecution.

I must say, in today's age and culture, the church needs to walk in such power. To declare the word, one must be bold. The world and its culture are hostile towards anything in the name of Christ. The truth is being rejected, and all those who carry out the "judgment" work (preaching the gospel) are being despised and rejected. Therefore, God is calling out to His people to arise in His glory. The infillings of the Spirit for supernatural boldness to complete the work are available. Yes, the world will hate you. Even some members of the "church" will ridicule the remnant that arises in His glory. But you are the chosen.

Thank God, the Holy Ghost indwells us. It is in Him we have access to the levels of God's glory. The infillings! The Lord has made available to us a never-ending availability of infillings. So, the Apostle Paul makes this command to the Ephesians:

"Do not get drunk on wine, which leads to debauchery. Instead, be filled with the Spirit." (Ephesians 5:18)

The usage of "be filled" in Greek here suggests that it is

repeatedly being filled. To be "filled with the Spirit." I stated earlier how "to be filled" manifests not only through tongues. However, there are many manifestations of being filled. Including walking upright and bearing fruit. It all is to display the glory of God. So, to be filled should be a part of our daily bread.

It is also safe to note that scholars noted the chapters in Ephesians starting from 4 to 6 to be applied. The Apostle Paul shifts from preaching (chapters 1-3) to application (4-6). Here in chapters 5:18, we are to make applicable to our daily walk In Christ, to be "filled" in the Spirit. Therefore, the "infillings" are to be embedded in our daily lives.

Remember Jesus our Lord, after being baptized by John, the Spirit descended upon Him. He was "baptized" or "immersed" in the Spirit's power. To walk and carry out the assignment and commands of God. But when He went into the wilderness, on account of being empowered, He was full of the Holy Spirit. Therefore, He followed the Spirit's guidance completely. To be immersed in the Spirit's power is to be "filled." To be "filled" is to be led. That is why being "filled" with the Spirit applies.

People of God, God wants us to be filled with the Spirit. It is accessible to you. For God to manifest His power and glory through us, we must first yield ourselves to Him and allow Him to take "preeminence" in our lives. Preeminence in our hearts. God desires to fill our whole being through His Spirit. But we must make "applicable" in our lives to seek the "infillings" of the Spirit.

"The Revelation- ll"

So, I ask you child of God; what say ye?

What is your response to your bridegroom?

What be your response to your 'Lord'?

He calls you. He beseeches you to answer.

He is looking for you in the garden He placed you.

He crowned you with glory and richness.

He clothed you with the endowments of a priest.

The best Wine (The Spirit) He offers to fill your belly;

And choice grape to eat of ease.

The time to seek Him early is NOW.

To know the levels of glory He calls you to.

"You are my chosen people.

The remnant in which I choose

I anointed you to be my witnesses

My representatives in the earth!

Therefore, come and dine with me,

So, I may refresh you with my choice wine;

So, you may be filled with my Spirit

So, you can be empowered to do my work

And walk in the purpose I called you to, as my bride.

The time is now. The hour is here.

To respond to the call. To say yes and be found by your Christ."

CHAPTER THREE

The Passing of The Mantle

Jesus, after being crucified and rising from the dead, He remained on the earth for forty days. In this time span, He appeared to over 500 brothers (1 Corinthians 15:6) and to His eleven Apostles; providing them with commandments and instructions about things of the Kingdom (Acts 1:2-3). Luke records that before He ascended back to the Father, He gathered His disciples and gave them one further instruction. The instruction that'll propel them into that level of Glory in Him, that'll enable them to experience the authority and Power Christ walked in. to fulfill God's Kingdom mandate on the earth. That instruction was for them to remain in Jeruslam, "and wait for the promise of the Father, which you have heard me tell you." (Acts 1:4). Jesus continues by saying, "For John truly baptized with water; but you shall be baptized with the Holy Ghost not many days hence." (Acts 1:5).

Jesus promised His disciples that not too many days from His ascension, they were to receive the gift from the Father. That once the gift comes upon them, they'll receive "power after that the Holy Ghost [the gift] is come upon you." Jesus through His instructions were preparing them for something. He was providing them an instruction that'll cause them to become mobilized and energized to complete a specific work through the empowerment of the promise. He was preparing them to receive the *passing of the mantle* of His ministry.

Jesus was giving His disciples instructions on how to position themselves in the appropriate place, to receive the Power, the authority, the mantle to continue to carry out His ministry throughout the earth. As witnesses of His through the power of the Spirit, their witness would be effective. Through their daily walk and preaching. Their witness would then be of Power through the Holy Ghost.

The Ministry of Christ Part One:
Relationship between Christ and the Spirit

One of the beautiful insights I received from the Lord while studying Christ's ministry was that the Holy Spirit encompassed His ministry. The relationship between Jesus and the Holy Spirit was one of single-heartedness. Yes, of course, Jesus is God manifested in the flesh. But it still amazes me how the Son of God is dependent not on His strength and power, but on the Power of the Holy Ghost. The Spirit of God the Father. I can only think about what Jesus responded to John the Baptist when he said, "I need to be baptized of thee, and comes thou to me?" and Jesus said, "Suffer it to be so now: for thus it becometh us to fulfill all righteousness." (Matthew 3:14-15). John remembered His testimony regarding Jesus, that He was the one to baptize with the Holy Ghost. That Jesus, the Son of God, is Israel's LORD who is coming; as John referenced the scripture of Isaiah the prophet, "Prepare ye the way of the LORD." (Matthew 3:3; Mark 1:2-3; Luke 3:4-6; John 1:23).

Yes, the words of Jesus to John the Baptist is ringing in my heart when I reminisce on the thought that Christ is dependent totally on the Holy Spirit. Jesus needed to do this; so that he could lay down a life for us (the church) to pick up. He lived a life as a human, without sin or blemish, trusted and dependent wholly on the Father, worked the works of the Father in the power of the Spirit, sacrificed His body for our sins, and rose on the third day so we could be justified as He is. This is what I think about when Christ told John the Baptist, "It becometh us to fulfill all righteousness." Christ fulfilled righteousness in Himself, so that we "the remnant can be righteous," and have the grace to walk as He walks, dependent on the power of the Spirit. A beautiful thing when you consider it. The son of God walked as a man, lived as a man, He ate as a man, and slept as a man. All so He could fulfill all righteousness and make accessible to us "the newness of life" in Him. Christ is the very blueprint that we, the church, should follow. After all, we are His body.

In considering Jesus' response to John the Baptist, I think about another statement Jesus made. In Matthew 5:17, Jesus says, "Think not that I come to destroy the law, or the prophets: I am not come to destroy, but to fulfill." Christ was stating to his hearers that He did not come to do away with the Mosaic laws or the prophets, but to see it fulfilled in His believers and followers. That Christ would fulfill it in Himself so that the life He poured out unto death on the cross would be a life of grace to fulfill God's law and righteousness. It is a beautiful thing really, that Christ retraced the steps of humanity back to the very beginning and walked perfectly before God without sin or blemish (that is why he's also called the second Adam; Romans 5:12-21).

This was the purpose and destiny of the "Messiah" from the very beginning. But you see, Christ chooses not to rely on his strength or authority to fulfill it, but that of the Holy Ghost. Why? To fulfill all righteousness and the law and prophets, he chose not to rely on his strength or authority, but that of the Holy Ghost. The prophets in the OT mentioned that God would anoint the Massiah with the Holy Spirit to do great exploits. For example, Isaiah states, "There shall come forth a shoot from the stump of Jesse, and a branch from his roots shall bear fruit… and the Spirit of the Lord shall rest upon Him." Then he continues to name gifts the Spirit will be endowed on Him, "the Spirit of wisdom and understanding, the Spirit of counsel and might (power), the Spirit of knowledge and the fear of the Lord." (Isaiah 11:1-2).

Another example is in a later passage of the prophet Isaiah (61:1-2), which says, "The Spirit of the Lord God is upon me; because the Lord has anointed me to preach good tidings to the meek; he has sent me to bind up the brokenhearted, to proclaim liberty to the captives, and the opening of the prison to them that are bound; to proclaim the acceptable year of the LORD.." The prophet stated that the Spirit of God would rest on the Anointed one, to do mighty things! Many other Old Testament passages also speak of Jesus' ministry filled with the power of the Spirit. It was the fulfillment of scripture, and to show that God validated His Son. That Jesus is the true King.

When our Christ was born, Matthew and Luke explicitly recount His birth. His birth resulted from a miraculous deed of God. The two gospels declare that the Holy Spirit conceived Him and that He was born of the virgin Mary. The angel Gabriel says in Luke 1: 36, "The Holy Ghost shall come upon thee, and the power of the Highest shall overshadow thee.." and continues by saying, "Therefore that 'holy' thing which shall be born of thee..." (verse 37). Because Jesus was born by the power of the Holy Spirit, He was holy. He was perfect. From birth, he was without sin or blemish. He was indeed the Son of God. Therefore, even from His birth, there was a unique relationship between the Spirit and our Christ. The purpose and mission of Christ were foretold, stating that He would have the Power of YAHWEH'S Spirit upon Him. From the time in the womb to the point of His ministry, He knew the importance of having the aid of His Father's Spirit.

Jesus relied on the Holy Spirit to fulfill what was written about him. Jesus depended on the Holy Spirit to fulfill what was written about Him, including "fulfilling all righteousness" and "fulfilling the law and the prophets." Christ made it possible that we could live a life in Him, controlled by the Spirit and filled with the Spirit to live a life of righteousness! To live out the law and the prophets! Being a royal priesthood means being in His kingdom of priests. To every one of us in the body of Christ, we have a ministry to fulfill, and we can only fulfill it through the power of the Spirit.

Jesus was baptized in the Spirit

It is a beautiful thing to consider. How Christ is the perfect example for the believer? He has already walked the path that every believer is commanded to walk. While on this earth, Jesus, too, needed to be baptized. Even though he had no sin, he underwent baptism. Why? "to fulfill all righteousness." (Matthew 3:15). He went through the process God placed on Him to fulfill righteousness in us. But Luke and Matthew record that something supernatural happened once Christ received baptism. Once He had been baptized, the Spirit of God rested upon Him and anointed Him (Matthew 3:16-17). Why did the Spirit anoint our Christ? So, God anointed Christ with the Spirit to empower Him to accomplish the task given to Him as the savior and Messiah. To empower Him to fulfill all righteousness and the law and the prophets in Himself, God anointed Christ with the Spirit, so that we may be fulfilled. It is a beautiful thing to consider.

Jesus needed to be baptized in the Spirit to accomplish (fulfill) His ministry. So, yes, Christ also underwent the baptism of the Holy Spirit. We too are not exempt, because Christ passed the mantle of His ministry to us. The responsibility of making His gospel and Kingdom known to the world He committed that work to us. How do you think we can accomplish it? It's through the power of the Spirit, the wisdom of the Spirit, the counsel of the Spirit, the understanding of the Spirit, and through the fear of the Lord given to us by the Spirit. He gave His life to establish unto Himself for the glory of the Father, a nation of priests, and a called-out people. It truly is a beautiful thing.

Jesus was led-by the Spirit

Luke picks up the story in chapter four after Jesus was baptized and filled with the Holy Spirit. In the next chapter, in verse 1, he states something very interesting. He says, "And Jesus, being full of the Holy Ghost, returned from Jordan and was led by the Spirit into the wilderness." Amazingly the bible did not say, "and after being baptized Jesus departed into the wilderness." No, Luke explicitly states that He was first 'full of the Holy Spirit' and was 'led by the Spirit' into the wilderness. Walking in the Spirit's power, Jesus was ready and equipped for His next task; and that was "to be tempted of Satan." This indeed points out another uniqueness of the relationship between Jesus and the Spirit. Christ humbled himself as a man, and dependent on the leading and power of the Holy Spirit. Even during His temptation, He overcame Satan through the power of the Spirit; through the will of God's holy Spirit, He resisted.

People of God, we are no different. The same precepts apply to us. Christ walked this journey as described in scripture to make it available to us. So, we can walk as His chosen people. To be led by His Spirit and walk in the power of the Spirit. Just as Christ depended on the power of the Spirit to resist and become equipped to fulfill His ministry; We should follow His example.

I'm reminded of the letters of the Apostle Paul when he admonishes the churches to walk and be full of the Spirit. In Galatians 5:16, he admonishes the Galatians to "walk in the Spirit, and ye shall not fulfill the lust of the flesh." The New Living translations say it like this, "Let the Spirit guide (or lead) your lives…" The scripture I reference in previous chapters (Ephesians 5:18) says once again, "Do not get drunk with wine, for that is debauchery, but be filled with the Spirit." The admonishments found in these two example scriptures and others, are no new law the Apostles laid. But they are just giving a command that was already given, through the life Christ lived. Just as Christ lived, we should expect to live lives guided by the Spirit and to be filled with the power of the Spirit. These are practical things Christ put in place and therefore trusted in the sweet communion of the Spirit. We should do the same. It is truly a beautiful thing. When you consider this divine relationship.

Many other examples in the gospels could discuss the relationship between the Holy Spirit and Christ as He walked the earth to carry out His ministry. But for the sake of the message of the book, let us continue to the next part of Christ's ministry. The ministry of Christ is one of Power. It is one of authority. It concerns itself with proclaiming the good news of God's kingdom and deflecting the works of darkness! Jesus revealed the outline of His ministry. Since He was the one who came in the "volume of the book" (Hebrews 10:7), the scriptures He preached testified about Him. A prophetic word spoken 3,000-plus years before His birth testifies to the outline of Christ's ministry. Everyone in his culture knew the scripture and the prophecy. In a time of oppression and turmoil, many were waiting and expecting for the prophecy to manifest any day now. In a quiet town called Nazareth, there Jesus stood up in the synagogue and opened that ancient scroll and what he read from it is very shocking.

The Ministry of Christ: Part ll

"Christ began His ministry"

Coming from out of the Judean wilderness, Jesus returned to Galilee full of the power of the Spirit (Luke 4:14). Luke tells us he was teaching in the synagogues in the Spirit's authority and power. Therefore, fame spread throughout the surrounding regions. This was the beginning of Jesus' public ministry. What our Christ taught and did among them we do not know from just reading those couple of verses in Luke 4, but my guess would be he preached the good news of the kingdom (Matthew 9:35). Now here in verses 16-29 of chapter four of Luke, we read Jesus enters his hometown, Nazareth. These people here are familiar with his family. They knew his mother, his father, brothers, sisters, aunties, uncles, and cousins. Therefore, this caused them to assume that they knew Him.

Now, the bible says Jesus upon entering his hometown went to the synagogue on the sabbath day. According to the gospels, it was his custom and tradition to interact with God's people and His word, by reading the scroll to the people on the sabbath. But He is now in his hometown. I can just imagine how the tension and mood that was in the room must have felt. Here you have all these people in the room claiming they know you, friends with your family, and to top it off, heard about what you were doing in the surrounding regions before you arrived (Luke 4:14). The anticipation and wonderment of what He was going to say must have been high.

The time finally came for Jesus to stand up and read a sacred text from the scroll provided to Him by the minister (Rabbi). The scroll given to Him was the prophet Isaiah (perfect). Jesus finds the passage Isaiah 61:1-2 and reads the passage:

"The Spirit of the Lord is upon me because he has anointed me to preach the gospel to the poor; he has sent me to heal the brokenhearted, to preach deliverance to the captives, and recovering of sight to the blind, to set at liberty them that are bruised, and to preach the acceptable year of the Lord." (Luke 4:18-19)

The perfect scripture to express the FLAWLESS MINISTRY. But Jesus, after finishing reading from the scroll and handing it back to the attendant, sat down to teach. The only words that came out of His mouth were, "The scripture you've just heard has been fulfilled this very day."

The portion of scripture Jesus read was a prophecy to the children of Israel regarding their situation while being exiled in Babylon. The prophet was not speaking of himself when he spoke such a prophecy. No, the prophet was indeed speaking of someone else. Well, who was he speaking about? When Jesus says to the people, "I have fulfilled the scripture you just heard this very day," He declares He is the fulfillment of the Isaiah passage. That the time for the Kingdom of God and the Ministry of the Massiah was at hand.

The Jewish people of that time knew that this passage of Isaiah had not completely accomplished its fulfillment when they were released from Babylon because they were still oppressed. They were, of course, under the Roman Empire's rulership and oppression. They've experienced sacrilege and desecration. Local towns were burned down, and villages were destroyed at the hands of these rulers. They were indeed in a state of oppression. Here stands a son of a carpenter, telling them that He was promised to them of old. Yes, this carpenter was much more. He was the "Visitation" promised to them from the ancient scriptures to come. He was the one who had God's government on His shoulders to display the Kingdom of God here on earth. This was the will of God. The ministry of the Christ (the anointed one). The

Glory of God.

The Ministry of Christ Part ll:
"The outline of Christ Ministry"

Once again, the relationship between the Spirit and our Christ is clear in the Isaiah passage, specifically in the first line that declares Jesus' ministry with the words, 'The Spirit of the Lord is upon me because he has anointed me...'. The Spirit of the Lord anointed Him, empowered Him, and graced Him to carry out the work attributed to Him from the beginning. Remarkable is the work of The Massiah. The Spirit is one with the ministry of Christ, His work, and testimony. It has to be, as the Spirit supernaturally reveals God's Kingdom here on the earth!

With considering the name "Massiah" or "Christ", we see Jesus as the fulfillment of this role. We can see that these two names mean the same thing, but they are spelled differently as they come from two different language classes. "Massiah" or in Hebrew "Mashiach" means anointed one or chosen one. Its Greek equivalent (transliterated from the Septuagint) is the word Christos, which means Christ. In the NT (New Testament), it is very often you'll see phrases such as "Jesus Christ". For example, 1 Corinthians 8:6 says, "And one Lord Jesus Christ, by whom are all things, and we by Him." The translation of such sentences is "Jesus the Christ (the Messiah or anointed one)."

In biblical times, people understood they anointed individuals for positions of authority in the land of Israel. In fact, in ancient Hebrew culture, it was customary to pour oil on the head of anyone who was being anointed. Mainly for those being placed in positions of authority. However, in ancient Hebrew culture, they used the term Mashiach to refer not only to one individual, but they used it for specific individuals in authority, such as the King, the prophets, and the priest. "The anointed one" was the term used by people in ancient Hebrew culture to describe these three offices in the land. However, it did not override the belief of the "Anointed One." The One true Mashiach promised by God through the mouths of the prophets, and as time moved on the Hebraic nation refreshed their memories of such ancient prophesies during times of diaspora (forced out of their land), being brought into captivity, and oppressed by powerful nations.

Now here in the New Testament (Greek) timeline, we are involved with the talk, dreams, and aspirations of the promised "Anointed One" coming at any moment now, to restore Israel. Here in our focal verse talking about the ministry of Christ, Jesus is declaring that He is here. The Anointed One, Christos, has now entered the scene. He is the King, prophet, and priest wrapped in One. A King as He is sovereign and Ruler. God the Father has entrusted into His hands everything, and He is truly majestic (John 3:35). He's The Prophet as He is compared to Moses. He gives law and command. He works as a deliverer. The priest, as He came in the order of Melchizedek the High priest, and offered a more pleasing sacrifice to God; which was His own life and body! He is the divine Son of God promised of old to usher in God's sovereign Kingdom. However, He did not come to usher in His Kingdom in the way they expected. No, He came to usher the Kingdom into their hearts (Luke 17:20-21). His disciples did not understand when he made that statement while He walked with them, but when He ascended to the Father, they received the Spirit of promise. Then they understood.

Jesus is the Christos! God sent Jesus to reconcile humankind back to Him. He is the one to bring them into His Kingdom (in His sovereign will). Therefore, He is the one that can bring us into "peace with God". Right standing with God. He is the one who brings us into God's righteousness. To be in His will, plan, and purpose! So, we mention the other components outlined in His ministry. His preaching of the gospel to the poor serves the purpose of healing the broken heart, delivering the captives, and recovering sight for the blind. The freedom of those who are oppressed and the news of God's acceptable year of favor. The purpose of His ministry and message is to bring man into God's "peace." That in His peace entails these significant benefits.

Christos-the anointed One

The first line in the Isaiah passage that outlines Jesus' ministry is, "The Spirit of the Lord is upon me, because he hath anointed me..." Once again, we see the relationship between the Spirit and our Christ. The Spirit of the Lord anointed Him, empowered Him, graced Him to carry out the work attributed to Him from the beginning. The work of the Massiah. It seems that the ministry of Christ, His work, and testimony is one with the Spirit. It has to be, as the Spirit supernaturally reveals God's Kingdom here on the earth!

With considering the name "Massiah" or "Christ", we see that Jesus is the fulfillment of this role. These two names of course mean the same but are spelled differently as they stem from two different language classes. "Massiah" or in Hebrew "Mashiach" means *anointed one* or *chosen one*. It's Greek equivalent (transliterated from the *Septuagint*) is the word *Christos* which means *Christ*. In the NT (New Testament) it is very often you'll see phrases such as "Jesus Christ". For example, 1 Corinthians 8:6 says, "and one Lord Jesus Christ, by whom are all things, and we by Him." The rendering of such sentences is "Jesus the Christ (the Massiah or anointed one).

In biblical times, it was understood that people were anointed for positions of authority in the land of Israel. In fact, in ancient Hebrew cultural it was customary to pour oil on the head of anyone who was being anointed. Mainly for those being placed in positions of authority. However, in ancient Hebrew cultural the term ment while He walked with them, but when He ascended to the Father, and they received the Spirit of promised. Then they understood.

Jesus is the *Christos!* The one who was sent by God to reconcile humankind back to Him. He is the one to bring them into His Kingdom (in His sovereign will). This is why He is the one that can bring us into "peace with God". Right standing with God. He is the one who brings us into God's righteousness. To be in His will, plan, and purpose! This is why the other components outlined in His ministry are mentioned. The purpose of Him preaching the gospel to the poor, the healing of the broken heart, deliverance of the captives and recovering sight to the blind. The freedom of them that are oppressed and the news of God's acceptable year of favor. The purpose of His ministry and message is to bring man into God's "peace." That in His peace entails these great benefits.

"The Oil Flows"

How does this apply to us? It applies to us in the simple fact that we are His "Body". He is the head of the Body. The Apostle Paul talks about in 1 Corinthians 12:12-27 how we are the body of Christ. Now, the Oil that flowed on Jesus flows on us as well. The same Spirit (who was the oil) that anointed Him, anointed us as well. So, as the oil was poured on the head, it flowed down to the forehead, to the chin, and then the beard. Next, it flows down to the very skirt that girds the body (Psalm 133). If you are in Christ and the Spirit dwells in you, you are anointed. You are commissioned to complete the same work outlined in Luke 4 that Christ accomplished. The oil flows to you too.

We are called to walk in the flow of the Oil. The oil that drenched our Christ. He calls us to walk in His ministry in the power of the Spirit. So that the gospel can be preached to those who are poor; to heal the broken-hearted, to proclaim deliverance to the captives, to recover the sight to the blind, to set at liberty them that are oppressed, and preach the acceptable year of the Lord! We as the body of Christ are the chosen ones because the Oil of Christ anointed us to be a kingdom of priests also in Him! The oil surely flows to us!

As Christ's oil flows down to us, His body, He passed the mantle to us; and by Him passing the mantle to us, He committed unto us His keys to the Kingdom of Heaven (Matthew 16:19). That in the very ministry He passed on to us are divine keys in the Holy Spirit to do the things He did. In the same way, the Father committed to Him the authority to bind and lose, Jesus commits to us the power to bind and lose. The oil of Christ rests upon us His church to manifest the Kingdom of God to mankind, that souls may repent and turn to Christ. The keys have been committed to us.

Keys in Greek is pronounced Kleis, which also can denote or represent Power and authority. This is what Christos (The anointed one) handed to us through the flowing of His oil (anointing; Spirit). He anointed us to sit in places of authority and to carry out His ministry effectively. This is why we have no excuse. All we must do now is "sanctify the Lord in our hearts" (1 Peter 3:15). This is why we are called to sanctification and consecration in this hour. We need to allow the Spirit to increase in our hearts. To take preeminence so He can effectively flow as the Oil of Christ!

The keys Christ committed to us through the Oil are what authorized us to fulfill the ministry of Christ. The authority to bind and to lose, the Grace to carry out this judgment work. So, I appeal to you, my brothers and sisters in Christ, to flow in the Oil. To walk in the power and authority that the Christos passed on to us! The authority He delegated to us in proclaiming the gospel to "binding and loosing" is already a completed provision, because of Jesus' completed work on the cross. Yes, Christ's work on the cross provides the complete work of salvation. His work on the cross expels the work of darkness and makes God's righteousness available to all who believe in His Christ! Therefore, in proclaiming the gospel in the power of the Spirit, we'll find ourselves using the keys to the Kingdom. To bind and to lose everything, that's the work of darkness.

This is the authority of Christ's ministry committed to us, His church. The keys given to us through our Christ authorize us to bind demons and diseases and to lose prisoners of sin, addictions, and sickness from their bondage and captivity unto salvation. As we continue to examine more of the components of Christ's ministry, we'll see the authority of "binding" and "losing" portrayed throughout, and by discussing it hopefully, it'll encourage you to increase in the glory God calls us His church. That understanding that the ministry of Christ is in our hands, 'll propel you to fulfill the great commission.

"To preach the gospel to the poor"

After Jesus establishes who He is and who Anointed Him through the passage, He continues by stating "To preach the gospel to the poor". This was the first component out of five that Jesus addressed what He was anointed to do. Why He was anointed with such a ministry. The first reason was to "preach the gospel to the poor." The word gospel here in the text in Greek is Gogol, meaning "Good News." The usage of the word expresses sometimes the subject (The Massiah), the person who is transmitting the message, and the "giver" or "provider" of the Subject who the 'good news' is about (God). Therefore, Christ came to proclaim to the poor the GOOD NEWS of the one God sent, and the LIFE found in His precious gift. See, God in the past has always given men gifts. The gift of life, the gift of understanding, the gift of reasoning, the gift of building kingdoms, the gift of inventing things that are helpful and essential. So on and so forth. But the greatest gift God gave to humanity was His Son, and that through His gift is eternal life. Reconciliation back to God and having peace with Him. This is the Good News. It is the good news of the Kingdom, and that Jesus is passing out the keys to all who put their trust in Him, and to the poor, the good news is unto them.

What is the meaning of the poor here in the text? The word poor in the Greek is ptochos and is an adjective. It describes someone or something. Here in the text, Christ is describing a "people", and the people are those who are lacking in any area known. The areas of social, economic, Money, love, family, physical/emotional strength, the sense of vision and purpose, Joy, peace, happiness, spiritual richness, etc. Christ was anointed to preach the gospel (Good news) of the Kingdom to those who are destitute. The hard truth to this matter is that this applies to all of humanity. The reason is that we are all destitute in some way, and one thing I know for sure is that all of humanity has in common; that is, being spiritually destitute.

Even we, the "church", should know that we are not spiritually alive outside of Him. That it is the Spirit of Christ who is causing us to be alive spiritually. This is the Good News Christ came to preach and passed on to us in His church; Christ has now come to reconcile us back to the Father, which is the only way to be rich spiritually. We the people of God are called and commissioned to proclaim the good news of the Kingdom, that Jesus Christ is the way, truth, and life to the Father. Humanity was not created to be separated from its creator. Since Adam and Eve disobeyed God in the Garden, man has been in a destitute state, because sin enters our hearts. Sin separated us further from our God. It separated us from His life-giving presence.

But the good news is that Jesus, through His life, death, and resurrection, made it possible for man to be reconciled back to God. Not only that, but He has made it possible where us can obtain the gift of God, which is eternal life in the Holy Spirit. Another chance to no longer be destitute but to be whole and rich through God's Love, joy, peace, happiness, spiritual blessing, and richness. Here on this earth, it is offered.

In Matthew 5:3, Jesus begins His sermon on the Mount with these words: "Blessed are the poor in spirit; for theirs is the Kingdom of heaven." The poor in spirit are about humanity not being spiritually self-sufficient. Although Destitute and poor, Christ offers well-being for those who are poor in spirit, through having a relationship with Him. The Kingdom of God is extended to them. It is extended to all mankind. So yes, there is a place where the poverty-stricken condition of man can be wholly annihilated by the very Presence of Christ in one's heart. The gospel, the Good News to humanity, calls for man to recognize that they are spiritually poor and void; but God in His mercy and grace provided a way of provision and escape, and that way is found in The Massiah. The keys to entering the Kingdom are in Him. This is good news for the Poor.

Regarding Christ giving the Kingdom to the poor and those who trust in Him, Luke records such sweet words from the mouth of Christ. He says, "Fear not, little flock; for it is your Father's good pleasure to give you the Kingdom." (Luke 12:32). Mind you, a majority of Christ's followers were those who fit the description of the components of His ministry. Most of them were socially and economically poor, oppressed (spiritually, physically, and systematically), the outcasts of society, they were in captivity by sin or previously in bondage to demonic influences, they were either sick or previously sick but healed, and some was blind (physically/spiritually). Christ comforted them in this verse by speaking the good news that it was the Father's good pleasure to give and offer unto them the Kingdom of God. It is to be prized above all other treasures. For the Poor man or woman, having the Kingdom in their hearts will substitute their disappointments, stress, worries, etc with God's supernatural peace, joy, happiness (blessing), and most importantly, His Divine Presence that heals the broken man.

Here's another powerful thing Jesus teaches His disciples; "Not to worry about tomorrow." Not to worry about what you'll wear, where your next meal may come from, etc. The GOOD NEWS that Christ proclaimed to the poor is when you seek His Kingdom (God's sovereignty and heart). He'll make sure all your needs are met (and then some). Jesus instructs His disciples in Matthew 6:33, "But seek ye first the Kingdom of God, and his righteousness; and all these things shall be added unto you." By seeking God's kingdom and righteousness is to be seeking God's heart, will, and fellowship. Having a relationship with God through Christ is seeking His kingdom.

One thing that can be certain about Christ's paradigm we see regarding His message to the poor is that the Kingdom is more than life itself. It is more than the very clothes we wear, the food we eat, or the cars we drive. It is more than the house we live in, or the many lands we may possess. It is more than any situation or worldly pleasure the world offers. I know it may sound different, crazy, weird, or non-sensible, but the Kingdom of God portrays the true model of "reverse psychology".

The Kingdom of God is indeed much richer than the things of this world, and that was what Christ was communicating to His followers. Above all these other things, seek the Kingdom. Desire the Kingdom. See (experience) the Kingdom. Enter the Kingdom. To enjoy the fruit thereof, you must seek to know it and live it.

The Apostle Paul, when speaking to his audience in the Book of Romans, had to correct them regarding matters that were not important. The church in this community consisted of Gentile and Jewish Christians. There were contentions and arguments about whether the Old Testament law should be still followed or not. One of the main issues Paul addressed in this chapter was regarding the eating of meats the Law declared unclean (for it was a stumbling block for the newly converted Jews), and with the issue of the observance of sabbath holy days.

The Apostle Paul exhorted both sides by speaking on the matter of grace. Telling the Gentiles that they are not obligated to follow the requirements of the law, but to practice their freedom from it in a way that will not offend their Jewish brothers. Therefore, Paul killed the argument by admonishing them to show Love to one another. Paul says in Romans 14:17, "For the Kingdom of God is not meat and drink; but righteousness, peace, and joy in the Holy Ghost." The matters of the world (including rules and regulations) are not the fined definition or purpose of God's kingdom. The rules, regulations, and beliefs the gentile and Jewish Christians exhibited only created strife, division, and arguments towards one another.

But as God's holy people, we are not called to walk like that. We are called to walk as children of light by showing love to one another. Regardless of the difference between rules, regulations, and doctrinal beliefs taught by our denominations or assemblies. We are called to "Love". At the end of the day, as called out by people on earth, it is about the Kingdom of God. It's about our relationship with the Father through the Power of Christ by the Holy Spirit. It's about enjoying the grace and privilege we have by being in the right standing with God (righteousness). It's about walking in the Peace that comes from God, and true joy that comes through the Holy Ghost.

We are called to a dying world because the world does not know Him, and because this world does not know Him, the souls thereof are poor. They are spiritually destitute. However, there is a harvest of souls that are indeed ready to be harvested. People of God, it is time for us to walk as Kingdom people and show the Kingdom to the world. To show God's will to all humanity, and that is to annihilate their poverty (of their spirit). God desires to fill them with the abundance of the Holy Spirit, so they can no longer be poor, but rich and alive in spirit.

Can the world see you bearing fruit? Can they see the sweet communion of the Father and the Son through your life? The

Apostle Paul mentions in Galatians chapter five how the works of the flesh are evident and in opposition to the Spirit (who exhibits Kingdom behavior and glory). He names out the actions of the flesh to be, "sexual immorality, impurity, lustful pleasures, idolatry, sorcery, hostility, QUARRELING, jealousy, outburst of anger, selfish ambitions, DISSENSSION, DIVISION, envy, drunkenness, wild parties, and other sins." (Galatians 5:19-21).

However, the fruits of the Spirit are Love, Peace, joy, patience, kindness, goodness, faithfulness, gentleness, and self-control (Galatians 5:22-23). This is the richness of the Kingdom of God. This is a true virtue. Can the world see the fruit of the Spirit displayed in our life? Can they see a never-ending stream of abundant life flowing through you, around you, and in you? This is still preaching the GOOD NEWS. In the way you live.

Therefore, people of God we need to Preach this GOOD NEWS about Christ. He calls out to the poor (all of

"Sent to Heal the Broken Hearted"

◆ ◆ ◆

A single mother who goes by the name of Cornelia is struggling to care for two kids on her own. She took it upon herself to work two jobs, where the second one she just started this week is a night shift position. as she felt any mother would do. She is behind on her rent and her utility bill must be paid by the end of the day, or the city will terminate her lights. That morning while clocking into work, she noticed that the credentials she used to sign in kept reading "invalid". After attempting five times, she walked into the office of her boss to find out why her credentials were not working. Ms. Jane, who was her boss, asked her to sit down and asked her why she had been late to work for 12 days recently. Cornelia attempted to explain that she works two jobs to care for her kids and most mornings must make sure they get on the bus for school. But Ms. Jane fired Cornelia and handed her the final check (amount: $250).

Walking out from her job teary-eyed, heartbroken, and stressed about the light bill due by the end of the day, she called her mother. Cornelia and her mother had not talked in two years after a big argument. Cornelia was not that close to her mother. After explaining to her mother her situation, her mother refused to let Cornelia stay with her. After begging her mother for seven minutes, her mother hung up the phone. Crying in desperation, she gets in her car and heads on. Upon arriving at the apartment, she noticed the door was padlocked and an eviction notice on the door. Once reading the eviction notice, Cornelia finally broke down crying out, "Why, God, are you letting this happen to me? My kids God...oh my kids."

Once Cornelia was able to muster up some strength, she drove over to the shelter that takes in women and children. By God's grace, they had three beds available. So, she picked up her kids and stayed at the shelter until she could get herself back on her feet.

◆ ◆ ◆

Now, there was a pastor named Paul white, and he had a church in the same city. The name of his church was Life in Jesus' International Ministries. He often volunteered at the women's shelter, teaching and preaching the word at their Sunday morning worship services for the residents. The first Sunday that Cornelia was there, He preached a sermon titled "Jehovah Ralpha- The God who heals, even the broken heart."

One day he happened to run into Cornelia at the supper market up the street from the shelter. Upon noticing her, the Spirit of the Lord moved in his heart to speak to her. He asked Cornelia how she was holding up if she liked the shelter, if she had any plans, and even asked if she knew the LORD on a personal level. To such a question, Cornelia did not know how to respond. The Spirit of the Lord then speaks to Pastor white and commands Him to sow a seed of $5000 into her life. With no hesitation, he wrote a check and handed it to her. The Lord also commanded Pastor white to say these words to her while sowing, "I see your hurt and your pain. I know your trails and I counted every tear that fell from your eyes. I also see your heart. It's broken and I want to heal it." After doing what God commanded Him, He wrote down Luke 4:18: "He has sent me to heal the broken-hearted."

After he departed her presence, she looked at the check and noted the amount. Cornelia started crying and leaping for Joy. That night she meditated on the scripture pastor white gave her, and that following Sunday she gave her life to Christ. As weeks went by, she became hungry for the kingdom, and she experienced different levels of God's joy, Love, and peace. Although her broken heart did not heal immediately, it was mended together by the power of God eventually. She now understands that her trials are no longer just trials, but her testimony. She also now acknowledges that the pain she experienced in the past no longer has a hold on her. But she now understands that it birthed her into "Purpose."

Cornelia experienced a life crisis. Something very traumatic and heart-wrenching. I'm sure it strained her heart through depression and stress, as she knew she had two kids to care for. She had no support, no guidance, and no sense of direction. But the powerful thing is that during her crisis, God sent a kingdom ambassador to her. Someone who is "called out" and chosen for such a time as this. He was a believer and anointed to be a witness. He was the one who carried the passing of the mantle of Christ's ministry. He was "all of us". Every born-again believed. He represented all of us. Cornelia represents everyone in the world who is experiencing any kind of broken heart. God calls us to them.

The world is full of life crises, and many things tear at the heart of this world. Relationship heartaches, financial struggles, no sense of direction, identity confusion, systematic oppression, social pressures, etc. Heartache is everywhere. People of God, we are called to such people who sit in any category of heartache. God needs them and desires to heal every manner of sickness. Yes, even the broken heart.

In the scriptures, we can see God's intent for the broken-hearted. David in Psalms 51 writes about God's special attention toward the broken heart. He says, "You do not desire a sacrifice, or I would offer one. You do not want a burnt offering. The sacrifice you desire is a broken spirit (lowly heart). You will not reject a broken and repentant heart, O God." (Psalm 51:16-17). Why is it that God looks so intently at such people? Because their hunger for wholeness (which God only has), is great. They are lowly on account of suffering, and God can exalt someone with a lowly heart. James says it like this, "And He gives Grace generously. As the scripture says, 'God opposes the proud, but gives grace to the humble." (James 4:6).

Healing and wholeness are more easily accessible to those who know they do not have it together than those who think they do. That is why Jesus says this about the rich man: "It is easier for a camel to go through the eye of a needle, then for a rich man to enter the kingdom of heaven." (Matthew 19:24). A rich man thinks he has it together on account of his great possessions. Therefore, make him proud. But someone of a broken heart and lowly spirit hears about the Kingdom and treats it like pure gold.

That's why the Kingdom of God belongs to the broken-hearted. It belongs to the crush in spirit and the lowly of the heart. That is why GOOD NEWS is unto them as well. As followers of Christ, the mantle is on us to preach to such souls in the world. We need to be like Pastor white in the story mentioned above, by being sensitive to the Spirit and obedient. It led Cornelia to Christ, and she entered the Kingdom. She experienced the levels of God's joy, love, and peace, and her heart was healed! This is the call of God to the church. This is the glory of God.

◆ ◆ ◆

Cornelia experienced a life crisis. Something very traumatic and heart wrenching. I'm sure it strained on her heart through depression and stress, as she knew she had two kids to care for. She had no support, no guidance, and no sense of direction. But the powerful thing is that during her crisis, God sent a Kingdom ambassador to her. Someone who is "called out" and chosen for such a time as this. He was a believer and anointed to be a witness. He was one who carried the passing of the mantle of Christ ministry. He was "all of us". Every born-again believer. He represented all of us. Cornelia represents everyone in the world who is experiencing any kind of broken heart. God calls us to them.

The world is full of life crisis, and there are many things that tears at the heart in this world. Relationship heartaches, financial struggles, no sense of direction, identity confusion, systematic oppression, and social pressures etc. Heartache is everywhere. People of God, we are called to such people who sit in any category of heartache. God has need of them, and desire to heal every manner of sickness. Yes, even the broken heart.

The Prison that Satan has placed humanity through his enticement of sin entails a place not just of captivity and blindness. But also, one of oppression. Sin has placed on the neck of all of humanity the yoke of bondage and oppression. The Bible mentions two main forms of oppression, the same way there are two domains of captivity: physical and spiritual. When we read and study the New Testament, the Ministry of Christ combated the work of darkness. The kingdom of darkness seeks to abuse its power by not only bringing men into captivity, and into the prison of darkness (blindness). But also, to oppress them through the domains of the spiritual and physical realm.

To better make clear the way the Kingdom of Darkness oppresses humanity in these two domains, let me just list some examples per biblical truth forms of oppression. Some physical and spiritual forms of oppression are physical sickness/crippleness that are directly resulted from demonic attacks, emotional problems that result from demonic oppression (mental crisis, unspecified depression, any unspecified mental illness symptoms, etc.), and social/political oppression, narcotic addictions, alcohol addiction, etc.

I'm sure there are other examples that one can "name" that are physical and spiritual forms of oppression that are the results of demonic influences. The physical world (the world we know and can see), is influenced by a world we cannot see with our natural eyes and senses. Each form of physical oppression is influenced by powers that are dark and evil. Malevolent forces that control the airways of this world. The Apostle Paul declares in Ephesians 2:2 that the patterns that shape this world and society are controlled by the powers of the prince of the air. Humanity is controlled by this power, and there is only one way one can be set free from this oppression.

Jesus, in Luke 4:18, declares that another component of His ministry is to set the oppressed free. Christ was anointed to set all of those who are oppressed anyway by Satan's power free from his prison. Christ holds the keys to the prison doors that bind man in sin and influence the Kingdom of darkness. The very testimony of Christ is the legit authority and right, for one to be liberated from any form of oppression.

To the one oppressed by economic and social problems, in Christ is freedom. To the one who is oppressed by a broken heart or emotional problems, in Christ is freedom. To the one who is oppressed by the yokes and bondages of Satan's power, in Christ, there is freedom.

This component of Christ's ministry shows the Power Christ holds over all other issues that the other components previously discussed seek to address. God anointed His Son and placed on Him the mantle (authority and responsibility) to release and liberate the oppression.

People of God, this mantle has been passed to you and me. As Christ church, we are called to walk in the authority of Christ to combat every form of oppression. The mission did not end once our Christ was taken up into heaven, or the foundational Apostle's transition from the scenes. The call is still unto you. It is unto us. It is in our hands.

◆ ◆ ◆

A man who had a severe drinking problem found himself being unable to control his behavior. He always unseemly cusses out his wife and neglects his children. He stays out all night on account of being drunk at the bar, and too intoxicated to drive back home. Let alone remember where he lives. At the moment he is too impaired. One night, he had gotten into a huge argument with his wife, and while drunk, physically struck his wife. This was not the first time he struck his wife while drunk, but at least the 60th time. Tired of the abuse (verbal and physical), she separated from her husband taking the kids saying, "you need help Dom. Please get some help. Your sick and you have a problem."

Two months later, Dom lost the house he lived in. He allowed his drinking to consume and oppress him to the point where he would spend all his money on alcohol. Homeless and out on the street, Dom came to his senses one day after hearing a choir singing in New Birth first Baptist Church. Wearied, tired, heartbroken, and oppressed, he walked into the church, and set down in the back row. The pastor was preaching from Luke 13 about the woman who was inflicted (oppressed) by a spirit of infirmity for eighteen years. The pastor preached about how Christ was ready to "untie the yoke."

Dom thought about how he had been married to his wife for eighteen years, and in those years, he was addicted to alcohol. The Holy Spirit spoke to Paul's heart saying, "Are you ready for me to break that addiction from your heart?" Dom after hearing His words, broke out in tears and surrendered his life to Christ. Ever since then, he has been alcohol free for 15 years, and serving as a deacon in a church. Although he is still working and believing God to fix his relationship with his children, he is growing stronger in the Lord Day by day.

◆ ◆ ◆

How many people in the world, do you think has a situation like Dom? Ready and waiting to be delivered from whatever is oppressing them. Waiting to be set free from the "spirit" that is controlling them and leading them to do things that damages them and their life. As I have stated plenty of times throughout the book, there's a harvest of souls waiting to be harvested. People of God, it is time to rise. It is time to Arise and shine and show forth the Light of Christ. It is time to walk in the power of Spirit, to carry out Christ mantle and ministry.

Christ is calling out to the world. He is calling out to them to exchange their burdens and oppressive yokes, with His yokes. He says, "take my yoke upon you and learn of me." (Matthew 11:29-30). This great exchange will enable one to find rest for their souls, and liberation from the yoke that oppresses their life. It is in our hands.

To Preach The Acceptable Year.

During the time of Moses, and while the children of Israel was in the wilderness, God spoke to Moses and gave him specific instructions. God tell Moses in Leviticus 25:8-17 to release every Israelite who was a slave, every ancestral property that had been sold to return to its original family, and the land were to be left untilled so the rich could not accumulate wealth. So that the land can also be at the expense of the disadvantaged (poor). This was instituted to promote God's social and economic justice.

Jesus declared that the last component of His ministry was to, "Preach the acceptable year of the Lord." (Luke 4:19). The acceptable year of the Lord is also known as Jubilee. It was a year initiated by atonement. Before and after the atonement of the fiftieth year the trumpet would sound, and the time of release (and redemption) begin. The release of every yoke of bondage that resulted from social and economic oppression.

The Ministry of Christ promotes the will of the Kingdom of God, and God's will that the year of "Jubilee" and "release" has come! Christ atonement initiated this time of Jubilee. The time of the oppressed to be released, those who are captured (in prison) to be released, and those who are blind (in darkness because of sin), to come out of their blindness. The time of Jubilee is here.

Even to the many people who are oppressed by the social pressures of society. Racism, being faced with prejudice, discrimination. Even the struggles and burdens of economic pressures. Many people and families that are poverty-stricken and struggling to get by on account of the set minimum wage. The hearts of many because of these issues are broken. Minds are weighed and troubled. Dreams crushed and no vision. But Christ's atonement has made available the Kingdom of God. The Way to the Kingdom has been made, through Christ. The way to break such bondages and oppressive yokes.

Saints of God, the mantle to carry out even this component of Christ Ministry is in our hands. To preach the Truth of God's Justice through the message of the gospel! To declare to this hurting world that there is a Kingdom, where the power of God will break every burden and yoke that binds! It is in our hands.

Society is in bondage on account of the prince of this world. Because of sin that reigns in man's hurt. The system of this world is not built or controlled by God's moral laws of justice. This is why no consideration is being given to those who are socially and economically oppressed. This is why the society of this world needs to see the true Light. The true Light that brings about God's Jubilee in the lives and hearts of man! Spiritual transformation is the way to bring about the liberation needed!

God called Israel and chose them to be a nation, His royal nation of Priests, to shine forth His light and glory. He wanted the nation of Israel to be different by demonstrating His righteousness and moral Justice (through obedience of His law). This is one reason why He commanded them to release their Israelite slaves every fiftieth year. How many civilizations in time past were known to release slaves (as part of a governing system)? This was in part for them to reflect God's Kingdom will in the earth.

The same way that Israel was called and chosen to reflect God's glory and Kingdom will, so are we (the church of Christ). Through Christ, we the people of God are called to reflect God's will and purpose to humanity. To reveal the "heartbeat" of God to man. God's heart, will, and desire to release humanity from every bondage of sin, into His Jubilee (freedom).

◆ ◆ ◆

People of God, a beautiful thing was made known to me while studying the year of Jubilee, and how the responsibility to shine God's will for man to enter this Jubilee is in our hands. I'm sure all of us who are truly in Christ, first came to Him broken, in bondage, and in sin. We thought we knew love but truly did not. The first couple components mentioned early (being poor, brokenhearted, etc). We were indeed bound to sin. But when we found Christ, He caused us to find a brand-new family. A family of believers who helped us to grow in Christ and even supported us when we needed help. This is what the body of Christ is.

The Ekklisia (a called-out assembly) of God. The Ekklisia of Christ is also a living organism. It is a community of believers. Therefore, the same way we were shown grace before and after getting saved, to find a new family. God has saved us to be a community, that welcomes all those who accept Christ. Those who are even socially and economically oppressed. God called us out to shine forth His glory and light, to this dark and hurting world. This was the mission of Christ. To call out to the lost and hurt and offer the GREATEST GIFT that can ever be attained. Eternal Life, and eternal life is knowing the father and the Son (John 17:3).

The glory of God we are to show forth, is the glory of being liberated from the bondage of sin. The way to show that is to walk in the power of the Spirit, and Christ Love. To walk in the Love that'll enable us to love one another. To be one and walk in the spirit of unity. This is the glory of God.

The mantle of Christ Ministry is in our hands. The responsibility to not only preach God's justice through the gospel. But to live it! The Apostle Paul declares that we are epistles to be read by man daily (2 Corinthians 3:2-3). What better letter to be read, then one that talks about God's Love in a dark and unjust world. People of God, this is why we should walk in Love to one another and walk in Unity.

Another beautiful thing I must mention regarding the mantle of Christ Ministry, is what James mentioned about what a pure and undefiled religion is. He says, "Pure religion and undefiled before God and the Father is this, to visit the fatherless and widows in their affliction, and to keep himself unspotted from the world." (James 1:27). The fatherless and widows are a group of people in society, who were socially oppressed and not even considered. But as followers of Christ, as the body and church of His, we should intend to them. Why, to show them the Kingdom of God. The Love of God. So that they too may be spiritually and socially restored by the Kingdom.

We are called to be intensive of such people, and not cast them away. The poor (spiritually and physically), and the socially neglected and economically oppressed. This is the Ministry of Christ. To preach the year of God's Jubilee. Freedom from spiritual and physical oppression! It is now in our hands, to be the community called-out to show God's Love and justice. It is in our hands!

Revelation Lll

The Ministry of Christ did not cease when Our Christ was received into glory. The Ministry of Christ did not only belong to the foundational 12 Apostles (including Paul). The New Testament records many of the first century believers walking in the Power of the Spirit and fulfilling the Ministry of Christ. The Ministry of Christ does not only belong to the first century church, but the mantle has also been placed upon "you".

The spirit of evangelism is still alive. The need for souls to be brought into the Kingdom is still imminent. The components of Christ Ministry (in fact, Christ Ministry alone) fulfills the will of God, and manifest's the power of the Kingdom on earth. Christ tells the twelve in Matthew 10 for them to say, "the Kingdom of heaven is at hand," and continues by telling them to heal the sick, cleanse the lepers, raise the dead, etc. Some components of the Ministry of Christ to combat the works of darkness.

Paul in many of his NT (New Testament) letters mentions the many gifts of the spirit. How the many gifts are used to glorify God and of course edify the body. But such gifts are also the results of the Ministry of Christ. It has been given so the church can increase, by demonstrating God's power and backing up the preach gospel with His power. The Ministry of Christ is of Demonstration and Power.

It is in our hands, to carry on this mantle of Christ Ministry. It is in our hands to preach the gospel to the poor. The poor in spirit on account of sin and those who are socially and economically poor. It's in our hands to preach the Kingdom to the broken heart. It's in our hands to preach deliverance to the captives. Those bound by Satan's power. It's in our hands to open the eyes of the blind, by preaching the truth of the gospel and showing forth God's glory! So those who are in the Prison of darkness, can come out into the Light (truth) of Christ. It is in our hands to preach liberation to the oppressed, and to declare God's year of Jubilee! It is in your hands. It is in our hands!

Revelation lll

The Ministry of Christ did not cease when Our Christ was received into glory. The Ministry of Christ did not only belong to the foundational 12 Apostles (including Paul). The New Testament records many of the first century believers walking in the Power of the Spirit and fulfilling the Ministry of Christ. The Ministry of Christ does not only belong to the first century church, but the mantle has also been placed upon "you".

The spirit of evangelism is still alive. The need for souls to be brought into the Kingdom is still imminent. The components of Christ Ministry (in fact, Christ Ministry alone) fulfills the will of God, and manifest's the power of the Kingdom on earth. Christ tells the twelve in Matthew 10 for them to say, "the Kingdom of heaven is at hand," and continues by telling them to heal the sick, cleanse the lepers, raise the dead etc. Some components of the Ministry of Christ to combat the works of darkness.

Paul in many of his NT (New Testament) letters mentions the many gifts of the spirit. How the many gifts are used to glorify God and of course edify the body. But such gifts are also the results of the Ministry of Christ. It has been given so the church can increase, by demonstrating God's power and backing up the preach gospel with His power. The Ministry of Christ is of Demonstration and Power.

It is in our hands, to carry on this mantle of Christ Ministry. It is in our hands to preach the gospel to the poor. The poor in spirit on account of sin and those who are socially and economically poor. It's in our hands to preach the Kingdom to the broken heart. It's in our hands to preach deliverance to the captives. Those bound by Satan's power. It's in our hands to open the eyes of the blind, by preaching the truth of the gospel and showing forth God's glory! So those who are in the Prison of darkness, can come out into the Light (truth) of Christ. It is in our hands to preach liberation to the oppressed, and to declare God's year of Jubilee! It is in your hands. It is in our hands!

CHAPTER FOUR

"Arise and Shine"

Out on the sea of Galilee, Jesus is found on a mountaintop (or hilltop), surrounded by thousands of His disciples (Matthew 5:1-2). After having been proclaiming the Kingdom in surrounding regions, displaying the power of the Kingdom, many followed Him from near and far (Matther 4:25). Jesus' disciples gathered around Him, as He prepared to teach them what is known as the Sermon on the Mount (or the Beatitudes). Here Christ preached to His disciples the principles of God's righteousness. This sermon is the most PERFECT sermon that addresses human conduct. The Way that all of humanity should seek to follow: is God's righteousness.

In this sermon, Christ teaches His disciples their importance in the earth. He compares His followers to two essential things in the world: Salt and Light (Matthew 5:13-16). Why salt? Salt is valuable in that it gives flavor and preserves from corruption. Christ says explicitly to His disciples, "You are the salt of the earth:" (Matthew 5:13). Christ is saying to His disciples (us) that we are the only thing that is keeping the earth preserved and flavored. The world is full of wickedness, and darkness is abounding all around. The followers of Christ are the only remnant in the world, that should be preserved from the corruption of the world. That is why we should be a godly example to those who are in darkness. The Apostle Paul declares in Romans 12:2 to not "Be conformed to this world: but to prove what is good, and acceptable, perfect, and the will of God."

We as Christ disciples are called to stand out. To not give in or fall back into the moral decay and corruption in the culture of the world. We are called to Arise and Shine the people of God. What good are we if we lose our savor (flavor)? In other words what good are we if we become lukewarm and conform with the world? Christ continues by stating that if we lose our flavor and saltiness, we are good for nothing, but to be cast out, and be trodden under the foot of man. (Matthew 5:13). We should consider what Christ says to the church in Revelation 3:15-16 when He addressed their lukewarmness.

People of God, we are not only the salt: the only thing that preserves righteousness in the world, by walking in God's righteousness and displaying His glory. But we are the Light. We are not called to be "closet Christians" who hide our Christianity by trying to fit in and blend in with the culture of the world. No, but we are called to stand out and shine. By walking in God's righteousness and standing on His word. This is what being disciples of His is all about. Obeying His commands and following His blueprint of Living.

Christ says in verse 14 of Matthew 5, "You are the light of the world, A city that is set on a hill cannot be hidden." Christ compares the Light of His followers, to that of a city on a Hill. A city that is on a hill is elevated and seen as a position of spiritual elevation. In many places of the scriptures, the writers would refer to ascending Mount Zion or the hill of the Lord as places of spiritual elevation. Most of these scriptures referred to Jerusalem where the house of the Lord was. In a world so full of darkness and seem to be in places of "valleys", Christ has placed His church (disciples) in an elevated place. A place of spiritual elevation and authority. The authority to shine His glory, Light, and truth to the world (who are wandering below the hill in darkness).

The imagery here is beautiful. Imagine the sight of a city elevated on a hill, shining in brilliance at night. If one is traveling from afar, who would not stop at such a city to find rest? The first thought would be of curiosity because of the brilliance of the city. The second thought would be "Here's a place where I can rest and find nourishment." As Christ church, we are to shine as the city on the Hill. The world is poor, destitute, and spiritually malnourished. They are in a state of decay. Many souls are tired of wandering and only finding substitutes that momentarily ease their worries. We are that city on the Hill. Called to shine forth the glory of God. The richness of God. We are Salt and Light. It is time for us to Arise and Shine.

"The Glory of God has Risen."

In 2021, I remember the words the Lord spoke to my heart. Words that contain the plan of where God is propelling His church next. These words I hold dear to my heart, and the reason I'm compelled to write this book. The words God spoke to me were, "I desire to come down upon the Mount of the assembly of my church and be seen amongst my people." In a season in America (let alone the world), where everyone was dealing with a pandemic, God had a plan. The plan entailed the next phase. God is pushing His church.

If we look around today, we can see that things are not how they used to be. The same order of things in time past, appear as if they are not going to work. When you look out into the world and behold this generation of people, what do you see? Do you see people who have respect for things that are considered "Holy", or do you see a generation of people who don't? Can I tell you what I see? I see a generation of people (in the world) who are different from the generation in the 1900s and before. I see a generation of people who are far away from the truth and engulfed in a thick darkness. Mere words cannot move them. Tradition is not amusing to them.

This is a generation of people who are the "age of rationale and intellect." A generation that believes in "living your truth" and to believe in what's considered "reality." This is a generation of people where religion alone is not going to influence them. Therefore, the prince of this world has found a way to gain common ground with this generation. To blind their eyes and darken their heart to the Truth. He imposed into their minds the idea that the God of the Bible is not real, and His way is not valid. So, he has them believing in the Universe, intellect, in their self-truth (the corrupt nature of our flesh). This is the stronghold he presently has on this generation.

I remember the Holy Spirit spoke plainly to my heart when He was dealing with me about the agenda of the Kingdom. The very words He spoke were "The approach of the Kingdom of God to this generation is shifting, but my WORD (message) is still the same." There is a shift in the approach of the Kingdom of God to this generation. Some things that we used to do in the past will not suffice. This is the time when we will have to lose. This is the time when we will have to lose (untie) some traditions, and ways we are used to doing something's. For God to get glory in His house.

What used to work in the past may not work in this generation. The Move of God in this generation is more than likely not in the places that we were accustomed to in the past. The approach at this time requires a different kind of approach, and the Spirit of God knows the approach the Kingdom of God has grasped. Holiness is still right, and the precepts of God's word are still Holy. The Message is still the same, which is the gospel of Christ and His testimony. But the approach has changed. God is now calling for His glory to be seen in His church. That's the approach.

This generation is looking for a sign, of course. They are a generation who won't believe until they "see", and God is making a call to His people to allow Him to rest upon them. To Rest on their lives. To rest on their ministries. To rest in their homes. To rest on their families. God desires to cause His glory to rest amongst His people. So that the world may see that the glory of God has risen among His people and know the way to true salvation.

Arise and Shine

It's only fitting and right to say that God is doing something phenomenal in the Kingdom. The Lord is calling His church to that which is glorious, to that which is honorable and Awe-inspiring to the nations. God is commanding for His glory to Arise and increase upon the church in these last days. Amid this generation that dominates the world today. For His light must grow brighter in such dark times. Because the world is so consumed with darkness and wickedness, murder rates are rising. The Love of many has grown cold. Suicide rates are increasing, and depression has taken over the minds of millions, if not billions, around the world.

However, during all this, there is a people. A remnant whom God is calling to Arise and shine in His glory. God is calling out to His bride (the church). Such glorification that Christ is bringing His church into: for the glory of His glorious house. He is calling us His people to a special place in Him. A place where His glory Rest upon us. A place where we take upon a pure heart, to be sold out to Him, and allow Him to arise in us and take preeminence. It is time to Arise and Shine.

Even though Satan has a stronghold on the children of this generation, the fact that there is a mass exodus cannot be ignored. The suffering, pressures, and darkness of this world have created so many broken hearts. It has placed in the minds of many that their formal way of doing things has not been working; It's time for something new. This Mass exodus indeed involves such souls. They are ensnared in darkness. Bound by the shackles of sin. But for these things to begin, the people of God must get into place. Remember earlier I mentioned how the Kingdom has shifted approaches. We must position ourselves accordingly in the Kingdom. It is time for the church to Let God arise in the midst.

To the assemblies here in America, the call is unto you. It is time to become properly positioned to the Kingdom's agenda. The darkness that has overtaken the land, the abundance of wickedness we have allowed to increase. In our schools with our children. In our very homes, and even in most of our churches. We have snuffed out the truth (Light) of God, for a lie. We have suppressed the vocation He has called us to as His people, to become one with the culture. We allowed arguments regarding politics and governmental ideologies to separate us. We walked away from the GLORY Christ called us to (John 17:22). Now is the time for us to Arise and Shine. For the time of our restoration to this Great glory has come.

Isaiah 60:1-7, "The Glory"

In discussing the glory of God in the bible, is described in multiple ways of how it manifests. In one way, it describes God's splendor and majesty (1 Chronicles 29:11; Hab 3:3-5). Glory is so great that no human being can see it and live. The book of Exodus mentions this glory (Exodus 33:18-23). Moses asks the LORD to show him His glory, and THE LORD responds to Moses that He was going to allow His goodness to pass before Him and proclaim the Name of THE LORD. But THE LORD tells Moses that he cannot see His face, as "no men can see ME and live." (Exodus 33:20). The prophets demonstrate that men can only see this manifestation as "appearance of the likeness of the glory of THE LORD" (Ezekiel 1:26-28). To sum it all up, this manifestation of God's glory displays His uniqueness, His Holiness, and His transcendence (Romans 11:36; Heb 13:21).

Another way that the glory of God is expressed or seen in the bible is as the visible presence among His people, later called by rabbis the "Shekinah" (Exodus 13:21; Exodus 24:16-17; Isaiah 60:2). This word originates from Hebrew, meaning "dwelling of God", which describes the visible manifestation of God's presence and glory. Throughout the book of Exodus, we first are introduced to this manifestation of God's glory upon His chosen people. God's Shekinah was manifested in the pillars of cloud and fire in Exodus (Exodus 13:21), and later God refers to it as "My glory" (Isaiah 60:2). His Shekinah covered Sinai when He gave the law (Exodus 24:16-17), filled the tabernacle(Exodus 40:34), guided the nation of Israel in the wilderness (Exodus 40:36-38), and later filled Solomon's temple (1 Sam 6:2; 2 Sam 6:2; psalm 80:1).

A third aspect of God's glory is His Holy presence and power. The writer of Psalms 19:1 states that the heavens declare the glory of God. As believers, we understand that the Bible teaches that the creative world reveals God's glory and creative power. The Apostle Paul further discusses this in Romans 1:18-20 how those who are unbelievers are without excuse, as God reveals His invisible attributes and eternal truth even through the visible things of creation (the world). God's Power and even the truth of the GODHEAD are made known (Verse 20). However, because of the darkness that Satan has imposed in the hearts of men, and the blindness he causes humanity to walk in (on account of sin), this glory is hardly visible. The power in this is that people of God can freely experience this glory and Presence just through His nearness, love, righteousness, and manifestations through the power of the Holy Spirit (Ephesians 3:16-19; 1 Pet 4:14; 2 Cor 3:18). Therefore, the people of God can carry this glory to shine God's love, righteousness, and presence to the world.

In these last days, the glory of God is still present. The Shekinah of God did not only belong to the nation of Israel. His shekinah was not only limited to being seen in the early church. The Manifestation of God's glory is a clerical call for the people of God through all generations. The last manifestation of God's glory is when He reveals Himself as Redeemer. The goodness of God is shown in many ways to man. In one aspect, His goodness is shown by God being a provider, in another it is shown by God being a healer. But one predominant manifestation of God's goodness and glory is when He shows Himself as Redeemer. This brings us to the message that this portion of the book will seek to communicate the final revelation of God's manifested glory.

In these last days, God has spoken to us through His Son Jesus. The very expressed glory that God has manifested to the world is the very person of His Son. It is safe to say that Christ is the final revelation of God's manifested glory, and in Him is the summation of God's goodness and fullness of the Godhead (God's nature) (Colossians 2:9). The writer of Hebrews mentions how in time past God spoke through the prophets. He made known His revelations through the mouth of the prophets. He made Himself known through the pillar of cloud and fire. He made Himself known through the Red Sea crossing and the feeding of Manna in the wilderness. But now God has made Himself known through the Final and Complete revelation of His nature, and that is through His Son; and in Christ is the fullness of the glory of redemption.

    The glory of God's power of redemption is the Glory the church inherited in Christ. This is the glory God is calling His people to walk in. The Glory of Him Shining the brightness of His son through us, to bring souls unto Him. The writer of Hebrews communicates to us by stating, "Who being the brightness of his glory, and the express image of his person, and upholding all things by the word of his power," that Christ being the express Image of God, purged us from sins through His sacrifice and is now seated at God's right hand. Now, as Mediator, the Redeemer, and the one who baptized us in the Holy Spirit, we are called to walk in this glory. The glory of the Son. So that many may see Him shining in us and through us and come to the knowledge of the Godhead (of who God is; His nature), which is only through Jesus. This is how Christ Himself brought glory to God on earth by fulfilling His ministry as Redeemer (John 14:13; 17:1,4-5); And we as the church (who are in His Christ's image) are called to carry out this ministry. That is why Paul says, "And all things are of God, who has reconciled us to Himself by Jesus Christ and has given to us the ministry of reconciliation." (2 Corinthians 5:18).

    This is the glory that God desires to cause to rest upon His people. While the LORD was dealing with me regarding this great glory, He provided me with an outline and results of His glory resting upon His people. We must understand and, most importantly, keep in mind throughout this portion of the book that the sole purpose of God's manifested glory is so He can be glorified. The reason why God manifests His glory is so souls and lives can be transformed.

    One of the most famous scriptures we quote about our God being glorified is John 12:32. Jesus says, "And I, if I am lifted from the earth, will draw all men unto me." The Apostle John continues by stating that Christ was referring to His death (John 12:33). We know Christ was crucified. But we also know that God raised Him from the dead (Romans 8:11-13), and through His resurrection, Christ was glorified. God raised Christ from the dead, so that He may be glorified through Him: For God is glorified through Christ, by drawing man to Himself, to be reconciled to Him. Therefore, as Christ is the express glory of God in these last days, the purpose of God's glory manifesting is so that He can be glorified: and through this manifestation souls will come to Him through Christ, to be saved and reconciled to Him.

This is the expression of His glory. God is calling us to walk in. God desires to restore and revive such works of this glory in His church. There is indeed a remnant of fire starters in this age, and His glory is arising and shall be seen in His house! To bring the Mass exodus of souls to Him. That is why it is time to rise and shine!glory displays His uniqueness, His Holiness, and His transcendence (Romans 11:36; Heb 13:21).

Thy Light has come.

Now, I'd like for us to dig a little deeper into this prophetic message. The very message regarding God's glory rests upon His people. The scripture that will be used as the base of this message is Isaiah 60:1-7. The season and time we have entered in God's Kingdom, these verses form the basis of this prophetic message. The first couple of verses that I want us to focus on are verses 1-3 and discuss the first point of the message: We are called to shine the Light of His glory.

Verse 1-3;

The Prophet Isaiah composed his writing during a time of

hardship for the nation. The southern Kingdom of Judah found themselves in a spiritual spiral as they prostituted themselves over to idolatry. After King Uzziah died, the prophet thought all hope was lost regarding the southern kingdom as Uzziah seemed to have been the last stand of righteousness in the nation. But Isaiah had a vision of the Lord sitting on the throne, and there received a call to His ministry (Isaiah 6). Through a series of revelations and prophecies throughout the earlier part of His ministry, the Prophet begins to speak forth restoration and future glory of the nation in the latter. Here in our focal verse (Isaiah 60) we find ourselves in the section where the prophet speaks of Zion's prosperity and peace. The Shekinah of God returned to the people that the Lord allotted as His inheritance.

The nation of Judah was in a state of darkness. Oppressed by the attacks of Assyria. The nation was in a state of darkness, not only because of opposition but because of sin. They were in darkness and gloom because they neglected the commandments of their God. But the prophet foresaw the glory of God of old returning. He saw the glory that shined on the people of Zion in the days of her youth when she was in the wilderness. He saw the nation returning to the former glory and covenant with her God. He saw the nation becoming one with the Shekinah of God once again.

The glory that God called them to when he delivered them out of Egypt. The covenant He made with them when He said, "If you obey my voice and keep my covenant (agreement), then you shall be my special possession and treasure from among all peoples..." and "You shall be to me a Kingdom of priests and a holy nation." (Exodus 19:5-6). This is the glory the prophet has foreseen them returning to. The glory of being His "treasure and special possession" and "a kingdom of priests and a holy nation." A people set apart by God to show forth His" glory" to the nations. That man may see and turn to Him. to worship Him and be reconciled to Him. This is the glory of God.

There is a message even for the body of Christ. The cooperate body altogether. The same way that the prophet Isaiah had seen Israel returning wholeheartedly to her God. Just like the Prophet saw the glory of God shining upon the nation once again, is the same way I can not help but see the same thing for the church in this age and onward. A cooperative call to the assemblies (especially in America) to walk in this glory. To return to a place of purity where we can be sold out for Him. God is calling His people to Arise and Shine. The glory the first-century church carried the zeal and passion they had for God collectively (by walking in God's love, righteousness, and the spirit of unity) is indeed returning in these here last days. God, Is calling us to Arise and shine.

One thing we also must consider is that we can't shine the light for God in a place of darkness and gloom. We can't expect to shine for God when we find ourselves walking, talking, and acting like the world. Also, we cannot expect to shine for our Christ and portray His image if we separate ourselves from one another, and through petty arguments, cause divisions. God is calling us to arise and shine! The time has come for the bride of Christ to put on her priestly attire and show forth the praises of our God! It's time to Arise and Shine!

If we recall to our minds the word of God, we'll find that it is true that from the beginning, God's purpose was for His chosen people to be a light. It has always been His plan and will for them to be His nation of priests and holy nations. He called them to serve in His "holy mountain" (Ezekiel 20:40). Regardless of the darkness the nation found themselves in during the time of this holy scroll, and regardless of their spiraling state spiritually (on account of rebelliousness); the prophet saw hope arising for the nation. He saw the future as the glory of God returning. That glory was the Light coming to visit the people. To restore the glory of God to His glorious house, and for it rest upon His holy mountain. That Light was the Messiah (Jesus Christ).

The Messiah was believed to be the one to restore or redeem the nation back to God's glory through re-entering a covenant with their God. Saints of God, we know that Jesus is the Massiah and that He is the Redeemer. He is the Light that has come and will come again to Israel. But church of God I say to you prophetically that this is the time of the church visitation. This is the time of God to visit His people. Do not miss what God is doing. Do not be like the children of Israel who missed their visitation (Matthew 23:37). The time has come to Arise and Shine!

I know there is a lot that seems to be going on. Many assemblies here in the U.S. seem to be in disarray. It seems that darkness has overtaken many assemblies and congregations. I know we are in a time where you can't tell "a church organization" from "the world and culture thereof." Many people claim to be Christians, but there appears to be no fruit of the Spirit; to show the distinction of Christ from the world. But despite all the confusion and chaos, to the true believers, God is saying, "Your visitation has come. Your light has come." It is time to rise and shine. Stand up in the Power and presence of the Holy Spirit and allow the Glory of God to manifest through you and in you. There are souls tied to your hands. God has a mission for you to accomplish! There is a ministry assigned to your hands, and that is the ministry of reconciliation. It's time to Arise and shine.

Verse 2; darkness covers the earth

In verse 2 of Isaiah 60, the prophet mentions how darkness shall cover the earth, and gross darkness the people. When you look around and see the events transpiring in the world, it appears as if there is nothing but gross darkness. Crimes increasing and murders are occurring in places you never thought would ever happen. Such as school shootings, church shootings, synagogues, etc. The hearts of man are growing colder and stonier by the ages. The spirit of lawlessness is running rapidly throughout the world.

The demonic realm has taken a much more aggressive stronghold on society. But here's the secret to change; It is in the church. It lies in that power that is in you. The Power of the Holy Spirit, who is the Spirit of Christ. That is why I am appealing to the church of Christ in these very words; it is time to Arise and shine!

The prophet continues in the same verse by saying, "But the LORD shall arise upon you, and His glory shall be seen upon you!" The prophet was saying to Israel that while the world will be in shambles, God will arise over you to be seen in you. To draw the nations to you because the true Light is with you. This is the truth with us in the church as well. That is why Christ called us "the Light of the world." (Matthew 5:14-16). We are not to be hidden. We are called Arise and Shine. God desires for His glory to arise among us people of God, so that others who are in darkness may see and "glorify your Father who is in heaven." (Matthew 5:16).

Yes, God is even calling us into a level of glory that'll break demonic strongholds off territories. From off-street corners. From off the minds of those who are oppressed, depressed, and possessed. Yes, God is calling us to a level of His glory where His presence and power will manifest through us, to free anyone captive by Satan's power. It is time to Arise and shine.

What His Glory will Initiate

The Glory of God, when it is seen upon the people of God, will initiate something in the nations. The manifestation of the Presence, Power, and goodness of God will trigger something in the hearts of many beholders. It's going to initiate a mass exodus of souls to the Kingdom. The prophet states in verse three, "And the Gentiles shall come to thy light, and kings to the brightness of thy rising." (Isaiah 60:3). The nations referenced here are the people who do not know God. The nations of people who are not in covenant with Him. The people who are in darkness. In its proper context, the nation of Israel will not see the fulfillment of this prophecy until Christ's second coming, when He establishes His millennial Kingdom.

But you see Christ, through His sacrifice and glorification, established a body of believers in His image; and bestowed upon them the glory of Himself and the Father. The glory to shine as a Light to the world. In Christ alone is this prophecy fulfilled, and the body of believers possesses this light. It is now time for us to walk in this glory, to initiate the Mass Exodus of souls to come into the Kingdom. Christ has already initiated this prophecy by bringing many from around the world into fellowship with the God of Israel, and He is still doing it today.

This is the prophetic message God is speaking to His cooperate body. The call to Arise and shine, so that God's Light can be seen among us. To draw many more souls who are experiencing broken hearts, confusion, sickness, destitution, oppression, etc. into God's Kingdom. God is calling His people to Arise in His glory, to show forth the way to Him; and that way is Jesus Christ. Christ has opened the door to the Kingdom, to all that accept Him. He is the Light that draws the nations to the splendor of YAHWEH'S Light, and in this age, He desires to use the Church to display that Light.

This is why we must rise and shine. We must heed the call to break down the barriers we have set up amongst each other. Especially here in America. The nations will not come if they do not see no light! If they do not see any glory! I'm sure if we knew the number of people who left the church, refused to join the church, or did not look the church way on account of the foolishness they see happening would shock many of us. The arguing, hate, backbiting, and division among the believers. There is no unity.

What is this glory that God placed on His Son, and the Son placed on His body? In John 17:22-23, Jesus says, "The glory which thou gavest me I have given them; that they may be one, even as we are one." And what's the formula of the church being one? "I in them, and you in me." The next question is, what is the purpose of this glory? "That they may be made perfect in one," and "that the world may know that thou hast sent me, and hast loved them, as thou hast loved me."

The Glory of Christ prayed for God to place on the church's glory. The Glory of the Godhead (the oneness of the Father and the Son). What is the reason and purpose? So that Jesus may be made known through the unity and love of the church, and the world may come to Him to be reconciled into this Love. See, through the church, Christ's glory should shine to the world, the revelation of the Godhead (God's nature, and invisible attributes). Through the church, Christ should shine, so that many may come to Him and be reconciled back to the Father. This is also why in Christ is the fullness of the Godhead bodily, as in Him is the complete revelation and expression of the attributes of the invisible God (Colossians 1:15).

Therefore, to the assemblies of America, Arise and Shine. Put aside ideological differences and denominational differences. The time has come to Arise in the true glory of Christ. There is a mass exodus of souls in the world who are looking for Light. They grope around in the darkness. Knowing not which way to go. But the Church possesses the true Light. The glory that has been placed on us, by our Christ. It is time to rise and shine and become unified.ness of thy rising." (Isaiah 60:3). The nations referenced here are the people who do not know God. The nations no

"Look around and see"-

The glory of God rising upon you, His church, will not only draw the nations. It will not only draw strangers and foreigners who do not know the Lord into His light. No, but the Glory of God will initiate the gathering of your bloodline. When we position ourselves and humble ourselves under the mighty hand of God, we will begin to see incorporated in this mass exodus of souls containing our family members who do not yet know the LORD. Who is covered in this gross darkness? Your sons and your daughters are coming. Some of you, your mother and father, are coming. Your brother and sisters are coming. The outpouring of God's glory upon His people will indeed initiate the manifestation of the promise God spoke in His word, "He will be saved- you and your household." (Acts 16:31).

In Isaiah verse 4, the prophet Isaiah speaks prophetically to the nation of Israel, another glorious vision he sees regarding the restoration of the nation. He tells them to "Look around and see" that they assembled to them, and their sons are coming from afar. When Isaiah tells the nation to "Look around and see", I'm reminded of the instruction God gives to Abraham when he communicates to him the promise. In Genesis 13:14-18, God says to Abraham "Lift now thine eyes," and "look from the place where thou art northward, southward, eastward, and westward; for all the land which thou seeth, to thee will I give it, and thy seed forever."

The same way God told Abraham to lift his eyes and see, and the same he way he prophesied through Isaiah to tell Israel to lift thine eyes round about and see the promise; this is what the Spirit of God is declaring to you, His people. The glory of walking in His glory is to see the manifestation of God's promises in your life. Even the promises regarding the gathering of your bloodline.

See, when God saved you and sanctified you as His own, He set in His heart to save your whole bloodline. God has placed on His prophetic timeline to save everyone in your family. Those of you who have sons and daughters who do not know the Lord, the passage of Joel 2:28, still belongs to you. God indeed means exactly what He said when He declared, "and I will pour out my spirit on all flesh," and "Your sons and daughters shall prophesy." God will surely bring your children unto Himself, and even make them His witness. They too shall experience the glory of God rising among them.

"They come to you"

But you see what's amazing about this, is that when you allow God's glory to arise among you, your bloodline won't seek after no one else. No, but they will "come to you." If you choose to walk in truth of God's commandments and allow His glory to be seen among you and in you, your bloodline will see it; and when they see it, will flock to you. This is why you must not think that your family is not watching you, observing you, watching the way you walk in the LORD. Don't think your family do not notice whenever you increase in the Lord. Don't think they don't notice whenever you elevate to another level in God. They see the glory and fruit. They see you "shinning."

The prophet in this same verse states "they come to you." He informs the children of Israel that when Christ sets up His millennial Kingdom in Israel, the sons and daughters of Zion will flock back to Israel. "They will come to you." Why? Because "they will see His light." People of God, this is why God is calling to us in this hour to let Christ shine. To let His glory reign in our lives, so "they will come to you." If your bloodline sees Christ reigning in your life, they'll be drawn to the light and one day cry out, "what must I do to be saved." (Acts 16:30). However, this is the season in God's Kingdom He is calling us into, the restoration of the bloodline. Therefore, "Let your light so shine," so that "they may come to you," and "so I may save your household" says the LORD.

Increase in God's wisdom!

The stirring of the souls in this time is creating a hunger. The many people who are in this great exodus are hungry for the truth of the Divine. One thing that the Lord has placed in my heart regarding this season that is upon us is that many individuals are waiting to just hear the gospel of truth (although they may not be aware). The Lord is calling many people from the North, the South, the East, and the West to come and dine at His banquet. That is why I want to express briefly how it's imperative to increase in God's wisdom. To increase in the knowledge of His word.

Even when your bloodline comes to you. Your sons, daughters, sisters, brothers, mothers, and fathers, whoever they may be. When they come to you, do not think they'll come to you with no questions. They will come with questions, and those questions will be about the glory of Christ that shines through you. They will first ask you about the Christ you follow. The Christ who is risen upon you. Therefore, we need to eat the word at this hour. We need to study the words; because when they come, they come to be taught. To be disciplined, As God's people, we need to be ready to witness, and always

> *"be prepared to answer everyone who asks you to give the reason for the hope that you have." (1 Peter 3:15-16).*

The prophet Daniel speaks about those who led many to righteousness. In Daniel 12:3, he says, "They that be wise shall shine as the brightness of the firmament (heavens), and they that turn many to righteousness as the stars forever and ever." Daniel speaks words relating to the godly who not only testified through their living, but through their witness; and wisdom (God's logos; word) could lead many to righteousness. He saw their reward in the resurrection, in shining in the glory of God.

But may I say to your people of God that we can shine now; and through God's wisdom, can lead many to righteousness through our witness. This is the glory God is calling us into. To increase in His wisdom that we may not only live godly but witness by His wisdom (His word; testimony). It is time to Arise and shine. God desires to make us His people, the epicenter of

His wisdom. He's given us His Spirit and word, and the Spirit is ready to reveal more secrets of His word. He's ready to increase our understanding of His word. So, we may be ready to witness His wisdom and glory. It is time to rise and shine.

The church's purpose on earth, as stated by the Apostle Paul, is to reveal God's ultimate plan to humanity. In Ephesians 3, the Apostle discusses the ministry entrusted to him. Paul reveals that the mystery lies because the Gentiles are joint heirs and participants in the promise of Christ through the gospel. Paul made it clear from the beginning that God's plan went beyond saving Israel and involved reconciling the entire world to Him. Verse 10 states that the Apostle Paul claimed God intended to unveil His wisdom through the church to principalities and powers.

Saints of God, as Christ's church, we have a ministry. We have a vocation to fulfill. The scripture declares in 2 Corinthians 5:18-19 that while God was reconciling the world through Christ; He has committed to us (the church) the ministry of reconciliation. One way we can walk in this ministry is by walking and witnessing the wisdom (word) of God. So, we need to become one with God's word and increase in the wisdom of it. We are called to declare the Good News regarding God's saving power, through His Son Jesus the Christ. It's time to rise and shine.

My Glorious House

It is an amazing thing that God has done. He made us no longer foreigners and strangers, but fellow citizens with the saints. He made us fellow citizens of His household (Ephesians 2:19). Placing us and establishing us on a sure foundation laid by the prophets and apostles. The apostle Paul in this same chapter states that Jesus Christ Himself is the cornerstone, which in Him the entire building (the church) fitly framed together grows unto "a holy temple in the Lord" (Ephesians 2:19). We are that holy temple. We are also God's glorious house, on account of being a habitation of God through the Holy Spirit.

Since we are a holy temple of the Lord and a sure habitation of His Spirit, it is with certainty we are His glorious House. As mentioned earlier, the church's purpose is to display the manifold wisdom of God to all that exists (Ephesians 3:10). It is a fact that it is for the church to manifest and display the glory of God. The glory of God's plan of reconciliation and His plan of redemption through Christ.

I love how Paul says it in Colossians when speaking about the preeminence of Christ. In chapter one, starting in verse 9, He first shares his sincere prayer for the Colossians and starting in verse 12 acknowledges the Godhead. He first gives thanks to the Father, who "has made us partakers of the inheritance of the saints of light;" and then he mentions how the Father made us partakers. It was by "delivering us from the power of darkness and translating us into the kingdom of his dear Son (Jesus);" God, the Father first redeemed us and reconciled us unto Himself through Christ, by bringing us into His Kingdom.

Now, in verse 15, Paul discusses Christ's preeminence in all creation. Paul discusses Christ's preeminence in all creation in verse 15, explaining that He is the image of the invisible God and that through Him, all things were created. In verse 18, of course, he mentions how Christ is the head of the church, which is His body. Now, the head houses the brain; Since we are the body, we are to submit to the headship of Christ and align ourselves accordingly. We need to position ourselves to follow His command and will, and the word tells us that God's will for the church is to "fulfill our ministry" (2 Timothy 4:5). The ministry of reconciliation.

As His glorious House, we should honor the position He placed us. It is indeed by His grace alone that are we a part of His household and are habitations of His Spirit in Christ. Now, in this hour, God is truly calling us His people to align ourselves properly to His will. To align ourselves near His heartbeat. The Kingdom of God is advancing, and the LORD is moving phenomenally. I am telling you, people of God, the LORD is about to visit His people and glorify His glorious house on another level. This is not a prosperity gospel I am selling you; this is about God being glorified amid His people, so those in darkness may see the brilliance of His glory.

As darkness covers the world, and kingdoms are in turmoil, man is looking for a way to escape. There are a lot of souls that feel trapped and are looking for a way out. God is saying to you His people to arise and Shine. The glory that God is about to pour out on you, His remnant, will cause supernatural events to transpire. It will cause the nations to wonder at the explosive power of God that will take place in your life. It is time to Arise and shine.

In our focal text of Isaiah, the prophet states how that when things happen for Israel, their heart will swell and become full of joy. When God manifests the fulfillment of His word to them during Christ's reign. Prophetically, this is what's being declared to you. When the glory of God arises among you and breaks out over you, you will look and behold these things happening. You will see the mass exodus of souls coming into the Kingdom, the increase of hunger for God in the hearts of many, and your bloodline coming to Christ! These things will cause your heart to swell. It'll be like a great harvest! A time of increase and explosion in the Kingdom. This will indeed be a sight to see, and God glorifying His glorious house.

Abundance Of The Sea/Wealth Of The Nations

It is impossible for the favor of God not to draw the things needed. It is impossible for the favor of God not to attract people who are needed. We have seen examples in scripture of how God's glory has produced favor and blessings to the one it rested with. In Exodus 12:36, God gave the Hebrews favor with the Egyptians. So, whatever they asked of them, it was given to them. The Bible then says that the Hebrews plundered or spoiled the Egyptians. As God showed His glory and power among the Hebrews, they instilled fear of God's greatness. As the Lord declares in another place in Exodus, "I will gain glory for myself through Pharoah" (Exodus 14:4, NIV). The Lord did just that.

Another example in scripture is when God blessed the house of Obed-edom on account of the ark resting in his home (2 Samuel 6:11). Now, the Ark of the Covenant was where the presence of the LORD rested; and we saw through scripture that the LORD could only be in a place or handled by hands picked by God. Obed-edom was a righteous man who treated the ark with reverence. Therefore, God rested there and blessed His entire house. The glory of God drew favor to that man and his family.

One last example that we find in the book of Acts 4:35 is as follows. As the church grew, the Apostles proclaimed the gospel with remarkable power and grace. The believers were being filled with the Holy Spirit, also witnessing great power, and walking in unity amongst one another. The glory of God rested so heavily in the church community that they sold lands and houses. They laid the money at the Apostle's feet to distribute amongst one another accordingly. Because of this, the bible says there was "no lack." The early church was walking in the actual glory. The church was called to walk in (John 17:22-23). Because of this, the glory of God rested cooperatively and produced an increase. The favor of God was surely there.

This is the benefit of walking in God's glory. Allowing His glory to rest on you and flow through you. People of God, I say to you, lift your eyes and see what is on the horizon. The glory the Lord desires to cause to arise upon us. A great and awe-inspiring thing God is causing to come alive.

If you choose to arise and shine and walk in the fulness of God's purpose. You shall see the great favor of God. Just like the prophet declares in verse 5 of Isaiah 60, how the nations will bring gifts to Israel upon their restoration; The glory that will rise upon you will draw gifts to you. Yes, to the one who knows God has called you to accomplish a specific task; God is going to send the help and resources to get it done. God's great glory is going to arise among you and shine on you. Yes, God will turn the abundance of the sea to you and bring the wealth of the nations to you. He will provide the resources needed to glorify His glorious house.

This Is what it's all about. The glory of God becomes visible among His people. To draw souls into the Kingdom. How the church increases in Power and glory through their witnessing, God desires to manifest such grace in the assembly of His people. God desires to glorify His glorious house. Respond to His coming Light! Respond to the visitation of His great Glory! Respond to the increase of favor and grace. He desires to pour out on you! It is time to rise and shine!

To the one who feels defeated. To the one who feels like there is no purpose. I have some good news to share with you. God has a purpose for you. God has not finished with you. Child of God, He desires to show you the fullness of His richness in Christ Jesus. Now, you have been lying in the ashes long enough. It is time to rise and shine. Throw away the garment of defeat, complacency, and immobility. God is calling us to take upon the garment of praise and to anoint ourselves with the oil of royalty. Arise and Shine.

It is time for the assemblies here in America to put aside petty arguments and dissension. To take off the garment of hatred and division; and put upon the garment of love and unity. As genuine believers, let us remember that our foundation is built upon the same confession of our faith and doctrine of faith. It is time to Arise and shine.

The glory that God desires to pour on you to beautify you is not so much to put your name on a pedestal, but HIS NAME. The Name of Jesus. I just want to prophesy that when you respond to the coming of His Light in this season and allow the glory of God to rest on you, you will walk in places you never thought you would. The Bible declares that your gift will make room for you and set you before the great man. God will cause "kings to come to your light and the brightness of your rising!" God will cause people in high places to seek you out; once you position yourself to walk in His ordained purpose for your life. All for the glory of His name, and to glorify His glorious house. It is time to rise and shine.

The Revelation lV

In summation, God is bringing the church into a time where His glory will rise among His people. Some may say, "How can this apply to me and my church family? We allow God to have his way every Sunday. We prophesy, praise God in dancing, speak in tongues, and just have a Holy Ghost-filled time." It is good that your assembly is allowing these things to happen. But the glory God desires to pour out on His people is corporate and is on a greater level. You may have a Holy Ghost-filled time in your worship services. But the question remains; Is there any fruit being produced when you go throughout your ordinary week? Are you showing love? Are you witnessing the gospel in the power of the Spirit? Do you have fellowship with people who are of a different color and have a unique background than you do?

The aim of God's calling of the assemblies founded on faith here in America is to unify the corporate believers. Although many people may say that this is impossible, a time is coming (now is) when the church will experience attacks that will strip us from relying solely on one another. Even now we see many people who claim to be in the faith becoming one with the culture of the world. But the true believers, of course, are already being persecuted by society in the culture. So, God is calling us to another level of His glory. To return to the glory that the early church walked in; the glory of being one.

We can't blame the world as they are in darkness. They need light and we are that light. Christ has made us the Light of the world. It is time for us to Arise in the light of Christ. We can best show that by showing Love to one another.

Not only is this glory calling us to come together in unity, but to increase in God's power and glory. To witness and walk in the power of God. Yes, this way of life belonged not only to the first-century church. The body of Christ is a living organism. We are not a dead church, and the world needs to see that "the Living God" is on the inside of her. It is time to arise and increase in God's power, and to allow His glory to flow through us. By this, the nations that are in darkness will flock to Christ's light that shines through us. This will start the mass exodus of souls into the Kingdom.

Last, the glory of God will draw blessings and favor to those who respond to His light. Our visitation is at hand, and we need not miss this visitation. God will supply great provisions to the people of God to advance the Kingdom. To fulfill the ministry of reconciliation, God will cause the gifts He placed in you to make room and bring you before the great man. God will set some of you who are reading this book in high places. Remember, it is for the up-building of His Name. He will bring these things to you to bring glory to His name! God will do this to reach and save souls. To glorify His glorious House.

The glory of God will arise among us, to show forth His praises. That's what we, the people of God, are called to. We are called to show forth the praises of Him who called us. I will say that the dawning of this great glory will not only entail the things mentioned in this chapter. No, but the dawning of His glory upon His people will include an increase and constant flow of a life-giving river. A river will issue out from the people of God. Once again, God did not create a dead church in His Son, but an alive church. That is why on the inside of every believer, He placed this river and infused it with gifts and graces. That the world may see and marvel at the LIFE imputed in the saints. Yes, He did this so the world would see and say, "God is within her."

CHAPTER FIVE

"God is within her"

The River's Of Life

In the book of Ezekiel chapter 47, the prophet sees a vision regarding the glorification of God's glorious House. In the vision, the prophet sees the Temple of The Lord (God's house) and sees water issuing from under the threshold of the Temple towards the East. The man who was in Ezekiel's vision (an angel) led him into the vision, and in his hand, the man had a measuring rod. The prophet Ezekiel states that when the men led him eastward and measured about 1,000 cubits, he caused him to pass through the ankle-deep waters. But the man in the vision does not stop there. He goes out further and measures another 1,000 cubits, which this time was knee deep. I would have become nervous and a little scared because I could not swim. But in this matter, the prophet Ezekiel had no control; As the sovereign Lord was showing Him a vision regarding the future of God's glorious house.

So, the men continue by going out deeper into the waters and measuring another 1,000 cubits. The prophet records that the water no longer stopped at his ankles and knees. But now it was to his loins (waists). However, the measuring of the waters that flowed from the Temple did not stop there. The man went out another 1,000 cubits. This time, the waters had now become a river he could not pass through. The waters that flowed from the temple were no longer a stream or creek, but now a full-force river. Waters that were deep where the prophet floated in the water. Deep enough to swim in (Ezekiel 47: 5).

The vision that the Prophet saw did not end with just the measuring of the waters. But the Lord brought Ezekiel back to the banks of the river, and he beheld trees on each side of the river (verse 7). The men make known to Ezekiel the destination of the river and its purpose. He also makes known to him the purpose of the trees and what provides nourishment. In verse 8 he explains the River will pour out toward the eastern region and go down into the Arabah (the Jordan Valley) and on into the Dead Sea, and when the waters enter the Dead Sea the waters thereof shall be healed and made fresh, and wherever the River goes everything shall live. The River, therefore, will make it possible for fishermen to fish on the banks of the Dead Sea. This is what the River will produce and cause to "be".

The Trees on each side of the River will produce food for the nations. The Leaves shall grow in their season and bear fruit for the nations. These trees shall never fail to meet the demands of all those who eat from the trees (verse 12). The fruit shall be for food and the leaves for healing. The powerful thing about the "being" of the trees is that its nourishment comes from the River that proceeds from God's glorious house.

Amazingly, the prophet did not see the river coming from any government structure or the King's palace. No, but from the House of YHWH. The prophet saw the glorification of God's glorious house in time to come. As he spoke through the prophet Isaiah in chapter 60: 7, "And I will glorify the house of my glory." Here, in this same scripture, the prophet sees a time of Christ's millennial reign, and the glorification of God's Temple in that time. The healing and restoration that'll proceed from our Christ, while He is reigning on earth, will flow to all the nations.

But as I stated in the previous chapter, I'll state it again; Christ has already started the fulfillment of this prophecy. The prophecy of God restoring and healing the nations. Drawing all men back to Himself (of course, those who believe in Him). The River that is stated in this scripture is flowing today, and wherever this River flows, it gives it life. One may ask, "What is this River exactly?" Well, the bible makes it clear to us what this River is. This River is the Spirit of God.

In many of the gospels (especially the gospel of John), our Christ compared the Holy Spirit to this Life-giving River. In John 4:14, Jesus speaks to a woman from Samaria and speaks to her about the living water. Now, this woman was no saint. Jesus deals with her about her sin in that she had many husbands, and the one she was currently with was not her husband. However, she continued to talk to Jesus on account of curiosity about the words He spoke to her, and when He acknowledged to her that He was the "I Am" (while acknowledging at the same time he was the Massiah) (John 4:26), she runs to town to tell the others!

But Jesus, when first starting the conversation with the woman, says these words to her, "If thou knewest the gift of God, and who it is that saith to thee, give me to drink; thou wouldest have asked of him, and he would have given thee living water." (John 4:10). Powerful to think that when Christ came into the world, He did not come empty-handed. But He brought a gift; the gift being the River of life, which is the gift of God.

As the prophet Ezekiel noted how the River gave life unto the Dead Sea and caused it to become inhabited with life; This Water that Jesus offers produces the same result because it is the Same River. Jesus, in fact, in this same scripture of John 4, exclaims that if anyone drinks the water He gives, will never thirst again. But the water He gives will become a well of water springing up into everlasting life. The very water Christ gives will become a stream (like that proceeding out of the temple in Ezekiel's vision) issuing out of the belly, unto everlasting life. This was not the only time Jesus stated this.

In John 7:37-39 there was an important festival happening and it was the last day. At the beginning of chapter 7, we read the festival was the feast of Tabernacles, which is also called Sukkot. The celebration of this holiday is twofold. To begin with, it relates to the fall harvest. The second commemoration is where every Jewish male traveled to Jerusalem while dwelling in booths. This was so they would relieve the experience their ancestors who were in the wilderness experienced. The best summarization of Sukkot is habitation. From the Old Testament, we know that while the children of Israel were in the wilderness, God dwelt with them. No other time was perfect for Christ to declare this message than on the last day of this celebration.

Jesus stood up on that last great day of the festival and declared, "If any man thirst, let him come unto me, and drink. He that believes in me, as the scripture has said, out of his belly shall flow rivers of living water." (John 7:36-37). While celebrating a festival that emphasized booths, tabernacles, and habitation; Christ made one message clear from the Father! That the time when God dwelled not only with man but inside of man was here. The time when God wants to make you His habitation is now. How? Through the Rivers of living water, bubbling up from the belly.

The Apostle John does not leave us clueless once again about what this River is. In verse 39, he states Jesus spoke regarding the Spirit. The Holy Ghost will dwell in everyone who puts their trust in Jesus Christ. The flow of this Life-giving River is indeed in motion today. Christ has made it available through Him. Every one of us who is truly born again has this River on the inside of us. We are no longer dead, but our spirits are alive through the Spirit of God.

The imagery of the Prophet Ezekiel portrays in his vision is that the River, the trees, the fruits, the leaves, and the river flowing out to the East; were also an analogy to the Garden of Eden. Now, most of us know the story of the fall of humanity recorded in Genesis. Genesis chapter 2 verses 8-10 speaks of Eden and the garden planted in Eden to the east. There was a river that flowed from Eden to water the garden and then split into four branches to water the whole earth. In the garden, this River caused trees to grow that produced delicious fruit, and nourished and sustained the tree of LIFE and the tree of the knowledge of good and evil.

What I want to highlight is the symbolism of the River. This River too represented the very Life of God issuing throughout all the land. Before Adam and Eve disobeyed God, there was harmony between man and his Creator. God freely fellowship with man, with no barriers. The man was free to eat from the tree of life and live in eternity. Eternity in the Presence of YAH. But then there was the fall of man. The enticement from the serpent caused God to drive a man away from the garden on account of disobedience.

Separated from His creation on account of sin, God, being omniscient, devised a plan from the beginning of the world. He had prepared a lamb and slain it before the foundation of the world (Revelation 13:8). Humanity who no longer commune with God and had no way back to Him on account of sin, God prepared Himself a Lamb. His very own son, who came in the very likeness of sinful flesh (Romans 8:3-4). Christ, therefore, laid down His life for the sins of the world. He poured out His life even unto death (Isaiah 53:12). But He did not lay down His life just to keep it down, but to take it up again (John 10:18). This was His glorification!

Now, through His very own glorification, He fashioned God a Perfect House. He gave the Father His body. A temple where

His life-flowing River can flow unto all the world. Jesus within Himself restored the very state of the garden of Eden; by now placing it in the hearts of those who believe in Him. See, what the first Adam failed to accomplish, Christ accomplished it. He finished the work through His death on the cross and through the sealing of it all in His resurrection. This River, the life-giving river, flows through Christ. It flows through His body, which is the glorious House of God.

The Apostle Paul talks about what Christ's glorification accomplished. In 1 Corinthians 15:45, he says, "Thus it is written, the First man Adam became a living being (an individual personality); the last Adam (Christ) became a life-giving Spirit (restoring the dead to life)." This is what I am saying, that through Christ alone can that which is dead be restored to Life. This is on account of the Life-giving Spirit, which is the Life-giving River, that proceeds from God's Temple.

Therefore, the restoration of what the first Adam lost is restored in Jesus. To point back to the imagery of the Prophet Ezekiel, through our sin and rebellion, we were drowning in the Dead Sea. Choking on the saltiness in that body of water. But when we put our faith in Christ, the Life-giving River of God that is in Christ made us alive. We are now growing into beautiful trees on account of the River and bearing beautiful fruit unto the Lord. Fruit of praise and righteousness! Because of the River, healing now flows from within us. This beautiful imagery perfectly fits what the Body (the Temple) of Christ possesses. Now the question is, since we possess such richness from this River, do we keep it for ourselves, or do we share it? Do we keep the River suppressed in us, or do we allow it to flow from our bellies as Jesus said?

Let The River Flow

God has always desired to be seen among His people. God wants His people to make His life known. Christ did not establish a dead church, but a church filled with His Life. When you read the letters of Paul, he mentions the many gifts and the capacity of bearing fruit that the Gift (God's life-giving spirit) has placed in all believers. The purpose of these gifts and the fruit is to reveal the manifestations of His glory. The church is impacted by these gifts and the capacity to bear fruit through the Holy Ghost is so that men may see God is alive.

In Ezekiel 47, the prophet describes where the river flows from. He states the river flows from the Temple of God. I mentioned before how we, as the body of Christ, have become God's temple. The Apostle Paul asks a question in 1 Corinthians 6:19. He asks, "Do you not know that your body is the Temple (the very sanctuary) of the Holy Spirit who lives within you? Whom you receive (as a Gift) from God?" believers and followers of Christ, God has given unto us His Spirit. The River dwells on the inside of us. Therefore, it is needful for the well that is on the inside of you to swell and spring up as a River. Reaching the nations and drawing lost souls into God's River (God's salvation and life). In the same way, the prophet saw the stream and River flowing from the Temple, so God wants the River to flow from us (His dwelling, temple, and body).

Getting in the Flow

God has always desired to be seen among His people. God wants His people to make His life known. Christ did not establish a dead church, but a church filled with His Life. When you read the letters of Paul, he mentions the many gifts and the capacity of bearing fruit that the Gift (God's life-giving spirit) has placed in all believers. The purpose of these gifts and the fruit is to reveal the manifestations of His glory. The church is impacted by these gifts and the capacity to bear fruit through the Holy Ghost is so that men may see God is alive.

In Ezekiel 47, the prophet describes where the river flows

from. He states the river flows from the Temple of God. I mentioned before how we, as the body of Christ, have become God's temple. The Apostle Paul asks a question in 1 Corinthians 6:19. He asks, "Do you not know that your body is the Temple (the very sanctuary) of the Holy Spirit who lives within you? Whom you receive (as a Gift) from God?" believers and followers of Christ, God has given unto us His Spirit. The River dwells on the inside of us. Therefore, it is needful for the well that is on the inside of you to swell and spring up as a River. Reaching the nations and drawing lost souls into God's River (God's salvation and life). In the same way, the prophet saw the stream and River flowing from the Temple, so God wants the River to flow from us (His dwelling, temple, and body).

There are steps that the Prophet points out in the scripture that as Christ's followers, we can take to get in the flow. The Prophet first mentions in the measuring process of this river, it being ankle deep. The transliteration of this phrase in Hebrew means "water of ankles." It springs from a root meaning "to walk about proudly." The portion of the water the prophet found himself in was shallow, and he could walk about proudly. To better understand, think about a small stream that you can walk through. Where the water covers your feet and is up to the ankles. The stream is so refreshing that you can walk about proudly. This is what the prophet is referring to regarding the depths of the river here.

What do feet represent? Feet represents our walk and our direction. The Lord leading the prophet into this dept of the water first shows that he (we) must get our feet wet first. We need to align ourselves wholeheartedly with the direction God is leading us. To submit ourselves to God, and the leading of the Spirit. So, he may direct our walk in Him. This is what it means to get our feet wet. Let me make this clear, we cannot lead ourselves into the flow of the River. It's nothing we can do on our own, to cause the

River to flow. We need to allow the Spirit to cover our feet, so he can lead us first into the deepness of God. All so the current of the River can carry us. So, the Spirit can fully control us, for the River to flow through us and fulfill the Ministry of Christ in the Power of the current that the River possesses.

The prophet then states that when he looked up, the man (the angel) that was guiding him went out another 1,000 cubits. The man then leads Ezekiel up to where he is standing, and the water is now to his knees. Now not only were the prophets' feet wet, but now his knee was wet. What do wet knees represent? It represents a place of PRAYER. See, this is another position that we, as God's chosen people, need to find ourselves in. Not just positioning ourselves in alignment with His will and walking in the direction He wants us to walk, but in prayer. Praying opens our hearts up to become more filled with the Spirit. It enlarges our hearts to love God more. I'm not referring to prayers that are ritualistic or filled with voided words, but prayers that are spoken from the relationship. This is what it means to have Wet Knees. A Position of Prayer out of relationship with the Father. See, when we position ourselves in Prayer the Spirit will lead us deeper into Him. Because our feet our wet God will lead us deeper into His will, and because our knees our wet (in prayer) God will cause our spirit man to grow, to receive more of His Spirit He wants to fill us with! When you increase in your prayer life, God will increase the banks of the stream on the inside of you. Now your knees are wet and the banks are increasing. God will move you into deeper waters.

We see this through what He does next with Ezekiel. In verse 4, the prophet observed the man measuring another 1,000 cubits. Deeper into the increasing flow of God's River and Spirit. Now the man takes Ezekiel and brings him into the place he now stands. The water now was to the waist or loins of the prophet. The loins in most biblical passages describe it as the system of reproduction and pro-creativity (Genesis 35:11; 46:26; Hebrews 7:5, a few examples). God was speaking something in this passage.

The Mighty flow of this great river produces fruit. Whoever loins this mighty river touches will enable it to be proactive and productive. Therefore, we not only need wet feet and wet knees. But we need wet loins. Allowing this river to flow exceedingly from within us, causing the production of fruit!

This is exactly one result of this Life-flowing River causes to happen. It produces the trees that Ezekiel sees when he stands on the banks. He also sees fruit that grows on the trees and food good to eat. The life-giving River procreates. It causes those who are in it to produce and give birth! Therefore, God wants us to get into this River and allow it to flow. Allow it to flow by allowing the river to cause us to bear fruit. As I stated before, Christ is the life-giving spirit that quickens us. It is also worth noting that Jesus tells us in John that because He dwells in us, we can bear fruit. As the Spirit of God lives in us through our faith in Christ, the River is the source of the production of fruit.

The production of fruit is not unto our glory, but the glory of God. Bearing fruit will cause the nations to see this supernatural production and become awe-inspired. That is why some of you who may find yourselves in the River of God and are loins deep should not despise the warfare or pain you experienced or have. It was/is all to bear fruit unto God. The work God is producing in us, His people, is beautiful, because it is to show forth His glory. We need to allow God to continue to work so His River may continue to flow to someone and pull them into His waters! Let His river flow.

Now the man leads the Prophet out further. He led him out another 1,000 cubits where now the river was over his head. The Lord called him deeper. The river was so deep that his whole body was now drenched and covered by the river. He was now I can imagine carried by the current of the River. It was now so deep that he could not cross it. Therefore, he was so deep in the River that he no longer had any control, but only the River had control. What is the Lord saying in this scripture? God wants us to become so consumed by the River that it is no longer "I", but "Christ that worketh in me." (Galatians 2:20).

We, the people of God, are being called by God to be so lost in this River (the Spirit) that we surrender complete control to it. The prophet's mouth was now covered, so his speech was controlled. His eyes were covered. So now what he sees is no longer what he perceives, but the Spirit. His ears are now covered. Therefore, he no longer hears what he desires, but only what God desires! His ears are now filled with the word of God. The flow and direction of the Kingdom. The Apostle Paul declares in Ephesians, "Do not be drunk with wine, but be filled with the Spirit." (Verse 18).

We must learn to submit habitually to the leading of the Spirit, so He may flow through us. We can see such life examples through the early church in Acts. For example, the deacon Phillip was so controlled by the Spirit that the LORD led him into a desert out in the middle of nowhere. But the Lord was leading him to a eunuch to whom He wanted the gospel of Christ presented. This is the glory God desires to pour in His church. The glory of the flow of this river. Where His people are so submitted and controlled by His Spirit that the River of life flows through His temple (the body of Christ) into the world who are engulfed by the waters of the Dead Sea. This is the glory of God.

Flow into the Dead Sea

The Prophet Ezekiel then mentions how the River flows in a direction one would have never guessed. A place that seems to be meaningless. The prophet says that the River flowed down towards the Arabah (the Jordan Valley) and onto the Dead Sea. Why would a River with such life flow to a place that has no life and is dead? The Bible says that as the River entered the Dead Sea (the putrid waters), the waters in the Dead Sea were healed and made fresh (verse 8). The purpose of the River's flow is to heal and bring to life everything dead. This is the reason the River of God flowed into the Dead Sea.

What does the Dead Sea represent? The Dead Sea is an actual place of course in the middle east. A body of water that is so salty that there is no life in it. The waters are putrid and, therefore, are called The Dead Sea. But the prophet Ezekiel sees the Life-giving River of God flowing into The Dead Sea and healing the waters. This causes life to form in the waters and every living thing the River touches comes alive. The picture shows a restoration of God's life.

The world is the Dead Sea. Sin separates humanity and God. The prince of this world has man bound by darkness and sin. Therefore, man is poor in spirit and has a sense of decay on account of sin. They are drowning in the waters of the DEAD SEA. But God desires for the Living Waters to flow into the Life of every man who is dead in sin. God desires to revive men into His life by causing His waters to flow to them. People of God, as the temple of God where His River flows, we need to allow the River to flow. Into every community that is dying and wounded on account of sin. Speaking directly to the crack addict and drug addict. To the one bound by the addiction to alcohol and prostitution. To the one who is experiencing identity confusion and bound by the spirit of homosexuality. God desires for His people to get in the flow so His river can flow through us.

You accepted Christ and God's River flowed to you, healing you. So, God desires to use you for His river to flow. So, we need to get in over our heads. To get into the flow of God's River and become controlled by the current of it. The flow of it. To allow the

Spirit to fully lead us. This is the glory God is calling the church! To allow the river to flow into the places of the Dead Sea. To flow into the world.

The Fishermen on the banks

As the River of God proceeds into the Dead Sea, the prophet states that an abundance of Fish shall swarm in the sea. Because God's Life-Giving River shall cause the sea to be healed and made fresh. Therefore, this will draw fishermen to the banks, to draw into the waters to draw fish. This is a good sign, as it shows life is abundant in the Sea.

Hear me when I say to you that if we allow the River of God to increase in us and allow it to flow, it'll draw fishermen to the shore. The fisherman in this sense is a man who'll come to draw from the waters. So, by the Spirit, I'm declaring that if we the people of God allow the River to flow through us, it'll draw men in the world to become curious of this River, and draw into the deep. Jesus, in many of the parables, talks about how when a man finds the Kingdom, he treats it like a valuable coin, a pearl, or some treasure to be treasured! This is what the River of God is. It is the Kingdom. It is the Life-giving- Spirit of Christ. When we the people of God allow the river to flow, it'll draw men to the banks to fish thereon. To eat the food of life that it offers.

People of God, this is the glory of God. Do not be surprised when you take heed of the words and messages in this book, and you increase in the flow of the Spirit; that people will be drawn to you. This is because the Life-giving River flows through you. They'll see the Life of Jesus in you, and His presence on you. They'll see the glory of God working in you and through you. They'll become curious about this life you possess and ask you questions. This is the choosing to draw from the deep. To stand on the banks of this River, and fish for the food God River offer.

Therefore, in the previous chapter, I talked about increasing in God's wisdom. There is a Mass Exodus of souls that are coming.

Because of the remnant that is arising in Christ's body, who is not afraid to walk in the Holy Ghost's boldness and power? You'll need substance when they come to you. You'll need the wisdom of God. That is why we are to get in the flow of the Spirit. To be controlled by the Spirit. So, the Lord may speak through us, and use us for the glory of Christ. This is the glory of God.

It all bears down to this; God wants the world to see that He is still within His church. He wants the world to see that He is still in the "midst of her." That there is a life that still flows within and through the body of Christ. Throughout the New Testament, it has been expressed repeatedly how Christ is to be revealed through the church. The glory is to show that Christ is not dead, but very much alive; and that He is the way, the truth, and the life. Through the precepts laid out to us in scripture on how we are to walk, and how we are to love should show the world the depth of God's love. This is what it's about.

God indeed wants it to be known that there is a God still among His people. This is what He wants to be known in this hour. Many things oppress the world from the wicked ones. No man who is outside of Christ possesses eternal life. The life-giving river that dwells in every true born-again belief does not abide in those who are not in Christ. This is what God wants to manifest. All so man may realize and repent of their sins. Turn to Him and receive Life! That is why God wants men to see that "God is within her" (the church) and to see Christ and live. So, we should let the river flow, so the world may know that "there is a river that makes glad the city of God." (Psalm 46:4).

"God is within her"

THE GLORY OF GOD

(2 Kings 5:1-19)

In these last days, God desire to make known to the world that there is a "GOD", and He reigns over all that exist. He desires to make known that one does not have to settle for what the world has to offer. The pains of suffering. The darkness and evilness that plagues the land. God desire to reveal to those who are suffering from addiction of drugs and Alcohol, that there is a WAY out. He wants to make known to the one who may feel dead inside, that there is a "River" that'll make one Alive; and discover purpose! In these last and evil-days God is calling out to His church. To allow His glory to arise among them, to show the world that "there is a God in their midst" and "His WAY is the only way" that leads to true deliverance. God desire to reveal to the world through the church, that "God is within her."

For it is true that this Declaration belong to you, oh bride of Christ "The Day of your Beautification has come." With the same words that the Prophet Isaiah declared to the house of Israel in chapter 61:3, "To appoint unto them that mourn in Zion, to give unto them beauty for ashes." So, I declare unto you. The time has come for the remnant to arise out of the ashes and from out of the shadows. It's time for the Bride of Christ to take off her robe of mourning and put on the robe of Praise. It is time for the bride to wipe her eyes from tears of pain and rejection and beautify her face with the ointment of Joy. It is time for God's church to Arise and allow the GLORY OF God to manifest. So, the world may know that "God is within her."

As I stated before, so I'll say it again; It is time to let the RIVER of God to flow. It is time for the Bride of Christ to allow the Life-giving River of God to flow into the nations. To flow into the world. God's will in this hour and in these last days is to reach as many lost souls. God desire to bring as many souls as possible unto His Son, so that they may Live. So, they may receive His River and be filled with His Life. The world must know that there is a "River that make glad the city of God." There is a River that flows in the church, that causes her to flourish in God's Life. God want the world to see, so that they may be compelled in their hearts and turn to Him and live. But we the people of God, have to first get in place.

In the book of 2 Kings 5:1-9, the Holy Spirit made known to me a couple of things to share with His people. Four basic pointers that the Spirit of God enabled me to develop into a message. It is nothing more than an extension to the message that I've been communicating in this chapter thus far. The message being that God desire to manifest His glory among the church, so that the world may know "God is within her." Now let us deal with the text.

In 2 Kings chapter 5 the story begins with an introduction of a Syrian captain, who name is Naaman. The bible says that Naaman a great man with his master and very honorable, as the through his hands the LORD has granted victories to the king of Syria. However, all though Naaman accomplished great victories and was favored by the King of Syrian, he had a problem. Naaman had leprosy.

With Naaman having Leprosy, it must had bothered him for some time because a maid who was a Hebrew spoke to Naaman wife informing her about the prophet in Israel. After Naaman's wife sharing this news with him, Naaman goes to the King of Syria (who is not named) and share this news with the King. Upon hearing this, the King gave his blessing for Naaman to go to Israel to seek out the prophet. He provided Naaman with silver, and six thousand pieces of gold, and ten changes of raiment to give to the prophet. The King also sent a letter before Naaman to the King of Israel.

When the Letter came into the hands of the King of Israel and he read it, he rent his clothes and said, "Am I God, to Kill and to make alive, that this man doeth send unto me to recover a man of his leprosy?" The king thought that the king of Syria was inquiring of him to heal Naaman. But that was not the case. The prophet Elisha heard that the king of Israel tore his garment. He sent a word to him saying, "why do you tear your clothes. Send him to me and he shall know that there is a prophet in Israel."

Naaman and the detachment of his military personals, traveled to the home of the prophet. The bible says that they stood outside of the door of Elisha expecting to meet him. But Elisha sent out a messenger to speak to Naaman. The commands the prophet gave to Naaman was not a command that was pretty or desirable. He tells Naaman to go to the Jordan river, and deep seven times to receive his restoration and healing. Now, Naaman was furious stating, "behold I thought, He will surely come out to me, and stand, and call on the name of the LORD HIS GOD, and strike his hand over the place, and heal the leprosy." Then Naaman continue by stating that the waters in Abana and Pharpar, and the rivers of Damascus are much cleaner then the Jordan River. What the prophet commanded Naaman to do did not make sense.

But one of Naaman servants talked some sense into him. Stating that if Elisha were to have told him to do some great thing, would he not do it. Naaman took into consideration the words of his servant and dipped in the Jordan river seven times, and Naaman was made clean! Naaman was restored from his leprosy!

The Prophet's role in Israel

In the Old Testament times prophets in the land of Israel, was seen as representatives of God in the earth. They were the mouthpiece of God in the earth. Throughout the old testament, God would speak and use a prophet to provide guidance to his people. God used his prophets to rebuke Israel when they were going wayward. Whenever it appeared that the presence of God was no longer visible in Israel, the people knew when Go showed up. Why? Because a prophet would arise. In 1 Samual 3:1 the writer of the book clearly expressed how the word of the Lord was "precious". In other words, God's word was rare because there were no prophets in Israel at this time. God found Himself going through a toxic cycle with Israel during this time. With them disobeying God and He'll have to raise up Judges, who had to deliver Israel out of the hands of their oppressors each time. But each time God deliver Israel they would fall back into their sinful ways.

Here God raised up a prophet by the name of Samuel. Through the word of the Lord, Israel knew Samuel was established as a Prophet, as God was with His words. He was a visible representation to Israel that God was in the midst. If we were to find ourselves back in the book of Exodus, where the Hebrews (Israelites) was in bondage to Egypt. They were in slavery for 430 years. When God wanted to make His power and presence known to Israel, He raised up Moses. Through Moses God worked wonders to get glory out of Pharoah and the Egyptians. Moses left these finite words to the children of Israel when they complained about not being able to bear the GREAT GLORY OF GOD that appeared on Hereb, "I will raise up unto thee a Prophet from the midst of thee, of thy brethren, like unto me; unto him you must listen. According to all the words you desired of the Lord thy God in Horeb in the day of the assembly.."[6].

The church is God's representative in the earth

In the Old Testament there was the establishment of Kings, priests and prophets. But now God has established the church. The body of His Christ! Through the Holy Spirit we are the representatives of God in the earth! As God's representatives, people should know that there is a God in our midst, who can do the impossible. People should recognize that the Sovereign one dwells in the midst of us!

God wanted it to be known throughout the world, that there is a God in Israel. When the slave girl who talked to Naaman wife about the prophet Elisha, she was basically informing them that there is a God in Israel! Naaman and his wife would have never meet this God, if It was not for this Hebrew slave girl who knew the Power of the God of Israel. Being a daughter of Israel she knows of His greatness. She knows what God can do. Therefore, she was not ashamed to witness that there is a God in Israel. Saints of God, we need to take upon this mentality this slave girl grabbed a hold of! Witnessing to the world about this God who is in our midst! Telling the world of the one true God, that can heal the root of all problems; sin

In the bible Leprosy was a disease that demanded him or her to be declared unclean (by the law of Moses). He was considered to be physically unclean and ceremonial unclean (spiritual). Indeed, leprosy produces the same effect sin has on us. Sin causes us to be unclean spiritually and physically. Spiritually because we are not righteous. Our spirit is dark and stained by sin. Physically because sin can make us sick and inhabit nasty behavior. Naaman struggled with this same sickness. No doctors could cure it and no herb could treat it! But the slave girl witness that there is a God in Israel, who can heal Naaman from his incurable disease! The world needs to know that there is a God in the midst of His people, and He Is able to restore and make whole! "God is within her."

Christ has made us His people a Kingdom of Priests, and a royal priesthood. In Christ we are endowed with gifts and graces that bring glory to God! Gifts and graces that if operated through the Holy Spirit, will cause the glory of God to manifest through us. So that the world may know the one true God! There is indeed some Naaman's God want us to reach! Man, who are bound in sin from the ends of the earth. God want them to see the glory of God shining among His people and know that "God is within her!" This is message is the same and it is the same declaration that has been echoing throughout this book: "God is calling His people to arise, to reach the souls who are dying and decaying in the world." God desire to Move mightily in His church, so that they may see "God is within her!"

There is a River

Another thing that God want the nations to be aware of, is that there is "a River". In verses 9-14 we read about the Miracle God worked in the life of Naaman. After meeting the man of God, Naaman receives a command from the prophet to dip seven times in the Jordan River. Now to Naaman it sounded foolish and cruel. Naaman could not understand why the prophet would want him to dip in a River that was muddy, dirty, and nasty. The reason being was so that Naaman won't be able to boast or mis-place his praise by giving to another. God wanted to show Naaman that there is a God in Israel. God wanted to display His power in a way were nobody well be able to get the glory.

See, this is the place God desire to bring the church into. A place in Him were He's able to work in ways where others will see it and exclaimed, "Now I know there is a God, and He dwells in the midst of His people." Yes, this is the type of place God desire to bring His people. Where He'll work supernaturally, and the world will see and be amazed! God is doing a new thing people of God, and we need to align to the shift of His Spirit. God desire to work mighty things in our midst. All so that He may get the glory and draw as many Naaman's to Himself to save their souls!

In the minds of many people today, they are like Naaman. Their minds are convinced that you can't sell me to try this River (Jesus). They say, "I don't want what these Christians is trying to sell me." To many people in the world today, they view Jesus like Naaman viewed the Jordan River; muddy, dirty and nasty. Undesirable to be dipped in. But you see, looks can be deceiving. Remember what Jesus tells the pharisees in the gospel of John. He says, "Judge not according to appearance, but judge righteously." (John 7:24 KJV). Judging by the flesh can truly get one in trouble and cause them to miss God's eternal blessing! But Jesus also says, "no man can come to me unless the Father draws them." (John 6:44). This is why it is important we must allow the River of God flow. To allow the Spirit of God to flow! It is only through the Spirit, can one be convicted and eyes open up; to see the eternal blessing in this Water!

God want to show the world that there is a River in the midst of His people. a River that restores. A River that heals. A river that delivers and sets free. He wants to show the world that there is a River that cleanses and saves! There is a River. By allowing the River to flow, we are really walking in the Power of the Spirit. When we flow in this River God will be in our witness. Our words will become anointed. As I stated previously, when the Prophet Ezekiel found himself in the FLOW OF THE RIVER, his whole body was submerged. His mouth was submerged. Therefore, his words were overpowered by the River. God was on his tongue. When you are in the flow, your tongue and witness is now controlled by the Spirit! It's here you'll find this scripture to be true "no longer I but Christ who lives in me." (Galatians 2:20).

The Power and the Glory God desire to work among His people. All so that man may know there is a God within His church! I'm declaring and seeing this by the Power of the Spirit. God desire miracles that are considered "unnormal" to break out. Miracles such as withered hands being restored. Tumors being dried up. Those in wheelchairs getting out of them and walking. Blindness is being healed and lifted. Cancer cells drying up from the root. Rare disease being completely removed from the body. God desire to work some phenomenal Miracles in the midst of His people. The time is now. The time has come. All so the world may know that there is a River that brings forth the HEALING of God.

Be Humbled

In verses 15-17 of our focus text, Naaman returned to the prophet to pay tribute. However, the prophet did not receive the tribute. Instead, he says to Naaman, "As the Lord liveth, before whom I stand, I will receive none." But Naaman came up with a solution that was acceptable. He decided to offer up a sacrifice unto The God of Israel. That one the prophet was well pleased! He did not receive no praise for himself, for he knew that the glory belonged to God alone.

See, this is what I am saying to you people of God. When God work these mighty things through you and in your midst. It is not for us to become boastful and arrogant. Some preachers, pastors, prophets, apostles, and leaders has grown arrogant from the mighty things God worked through them. Some of them has grown fat from God's offering. The offering that man who saw God worked mighty through them, and brought gifts to lay on the alter of God. These man or women did not give to the Lord what was due to Him, but instead stole from the Lord what was offered to Him. Do not worry or think for a moment that they will escape, for God has a due process for them.

But to you oh child of God, you must be humble. Take to heart the example that the man of God displayed in this text. We are to be humble. To never take glory for ourselves when God uses us to move mighty. It is needful that we understand it is God who is doing the work through us. It is about souls. It is about God receiving the glory from those who come, to tribute it to him. We must be humble.

The word of God tells us the blessing in humbling ourselves. In James 4:10 it states that we are to humble ourselves before the Lord, and he will lift us up. God exalts those who are humble. The bible says that God resists the proud but gives grace to the humble (1 Peter5:5-6). To be humble God gives grace. He establishes His favor on the one who walks in humility before Him! God can genuinely use those and display His glory among them who walk in humility. Therefore, to those who walk in humility my prayer is that God increases His grace on your life! The grace to increase in the Power and strength of God! The grace to be able to be position so God can work the miraculous in you and through you!

The Revelation V

Since the beginning of time God had a plan. There has always been a body of people predestined from the beginning.

The Apostle Paul states that those He foreknew He predestined (Romans 8:29). When He first created man and placed him in the garden. God foreknew. From the time He instructed Noah to build the ark and He judged the world through a mighty flood. He foreknew. Even when He spoke to Abraham and promised Him that His descendants would be as numerous as the stars, He foreknew. For unto Abraham He says, "and in thy seed shall all the nations of the earth be blessed." (Genesis 22:18).

Through the generations of Isaac, Jacob and the 12 sons of Jacob (the 12 tribes) God still foreknew. In the time when the Israelites was in slavery in Egypt for 430 years, and God raised up Moses to deliver them out of bondage. In the wilderness God gave them the covenant that contained His grace. The shadow of the One to come. God foreknew. Through the time of Joshua, the judges, the formation of the Kingdom of Israel, and the period of the prophets. God foreknew. He foreknew because through 42 generations God was watching over a seed. A see that would one day become an embryo through divine intervention. The formation of a body that'll house the Son of God, and the very Covenant of Grace. Through this one man, those who He foreknew would "become" the sons of God.

In the very mission Christ accomplished on the cross by giving up His body unto death, He opened the door. He paved the way for many sons and daughters (whom God foreknew) could be born through Him. As Jesus declared in John 12:24-26 how one grain of wheat if it dies produces a manifold harvest. This was the result of Christ death and glorification. In Him God foreknew and predestined.

Who did He foreknow a predestined? You, the body of Christ. You are the ones who He foreknew and predestined. Destined you to be in His kingdom for such a time as this. You are the last day remnant whom He placed on the earth. The body of believers who are born of fire and blood. A remnant of believers God has predestined to walk in the fullness of God's Spirit. The time has come for you to rise and shine. The prophet Joel has seen the day of your arising. "a generation who the Lord will pour out His Spirit and make them His witnesses. Born of the fire of the Holy Spirit." You are that generation.

The time has come to carry out the mantle that was handed down to us, by our Christ. The mantle of the Ministry of Christ. He has placed it in our hands. It is time for us to fulfill the great commission by walking in the Power of the Spirit, He has given unto us. It is time, in the power of the Spirit to preach the gospel to the poor, heal the brokenhearted, preach liberty to the captive, recover the sight of the blind, open the prison doors, preach freedom to the oppress, and declare the year of the Lord's favor. The time has come.

It is time to Arise and Shine. To allow the Glory of our Christ to shine among us. Those whom He foreknew and predestined. It is time for the body of Christ to allow God to arise, so He may glorify His glorious House. God desire to fill His house (family) with more souls of humanity. God desire for His bride to reach out into this hurting world and show somebody Christ. The time has come for His people to arise and shine.

The assemblies in America have remained dormant long enough. We have remained divided long enough. It is time for us to put aside every weight and sin that so easily beseech us. The time has come for the assemblies in America to position themselves, to get in the Flow of God's River. The flow of God's Spirit. God desire for His people to be so consumed with the flow of the river (the spirit) that we'll be controlled by the Holy Ghost. Our ears will be consumed. Our eyes consumed. Mouth consumed. Our arms consumed, legs consumed, and mind consumed. God is calling the assemblies in America to get in the flow of God.

Most of our brothers and sisters across seas have gotten the memo. Their increasing and prevailing in the Power of God! Uncommon miracles are the norm in most churches across the way! But to the assemblies in America, God desire to move miraculous in our midst. He desires to revive in our midst uncommon Miraculous. The manifestation of uncommon healings and restorations! This is the glory of God!

God want it to be known that He is within His church! Here in America, in the assemblies He established He desire for the people to see. Too many people are broken in this land. God eyes are on these destitute souls. The time has come, and the hour is now! It is time for us to take heed to the Isaiah 58:6-7 fast. To lose the bands of wickedness, to undo the heavy burden, and to let the oppressed go free, that we break every yoke. It is time we return to that which is pure, holy and justice. It is time for us to untie every traditional ideology in our assemblies, that places a heavy yoke on the neck of fellow brothers and sisters. It is time for us to make amends with our brothers and sisters and put aside petty differences. Then when we take upon the spirit of repentance and reconciliation with each other, we'll begin to see a fire spread across the land. By the Spirit of the Lord, I believe however, that there is a remnant who is taking heed to what God requires from us in this hour.

BIBLIOGRAPHY

Barton, John, and John Muddiman. The Oxford Bible commentary. Oxford: Oxford University Press, 2012.

"Bible Commentary of the Whole Bible with Pastor David Guzik." Enduring Word, October 13, 2022. https://enduringword.com/bible-commentary/.

Evans, Tony. The Tony Evans Bible commentary: Advancing god's kingdom agenda. Nashville, TN: Holman Reference, 2019.

Interlinear bible: Greek, Hebrew, transliterated, English, Strong's. Accessed March 28, 2024. https://biblehub.com/interlinear/.

Life application study bible: New living translation. Carol Stream, IL: Tyndale House Publishers, 2019.

Rice, John R. The king of the jews: A verse-by-verse commentary on the gospel according to Matthew. Grand Rapids, MI: Zondervan, 1957.

Stamps, Donald C., and J. Wesley Adams. Life in the spirit study bible: King James Version. Grand Rapids, MI: Zondervan, 2003.

Stern, David H., and Barry A. Rubin. The Complete Jewish Study Bible: Insights for jews & christians: Illuminating the jewishness of god's word. Peabody, MA: Hendrickson Bibles, 2016.

Wommack, Andrew. Romans: Paul's masterpiece on grace: Bible commentary. Tulsa: Harrison House Publishers, 2021.

ACKNOWLEDGEMENT

I just want to thank first and foremost God, who given me the strength through the Holy Spirit to complete this assignment. Without His supernatural strength and grace I would've never accomplish the Task. Thank God for my Wife who encouraged me, prayed with me, and stood by me through the process of this project. Thank God for my pastor Dr. Dameion Royal for providing his wisdom and God inspired messages, that help me to fine tune the message in the book. Grace and peace to all of God's people.

BOOKS IN THIS SERIES

The Glory of God

In these last days God desire for His glory to be seen upon His church, in an unprecedented way. The time has come for the church of Christ to assume their positions as the Light of the world. We are an embassy that represent the Kingdom of Heaven on the earth, and the time has come for us to represent.

The Glory of God book series seek to exhort the body of Christ to arise in Christ. The series addresses issues that the assemblies (churches) in the U.S. face such as political issues, division in the churches, many churches being pulled away by the culture, many departing from the faith, etc. As the book series states throughout the message, "God established the church to be a Royal priesthood and a holy nation", Minister Demetrius expresses that the call for the assemblies in America to sanctify the Lord God in their hearts is highly urgent in this hour

Join Minister Demetrius Battle as he shares the prophetic words the Father expressed to him, regarding the church of Christ in this hour.

The Glory Of God: Volume 2

** Volume 2 is in the works, and will be released soon!**

To stay in the loop, follow the social media platforms below;

Facebook: @Demetrius Battle

Youtube: @TheWayMinistries

Made in the USA
Middletown, DE
20 May 2024